MIRACLES
TAKE A
LITTLE
LONGER

MIRACLES TAKE A LITTLE LONGER

Roy Harley Lewis

St. Martin's Press
New York

Design by Doris Borowsky

Library of Congress Cataloging in Publication Data

Lewis, Roy Harley.
Miracles take a little longer.

I. Title.
PR6062.E9543M57   1986   823′.914   85-26055
ISBN 0-312-53429-9

First Edition

10 9 8 7 6 5 4 3 2 1

MIRACLES
TAKE A
LITTLE
LONGER

Deserted, the bindery presented a sweeping landscape of books and equipment suspended in time by the artificiality of the lunch break. In various stages of completion, uneven piles of books stacked on benches were like miniature mountain ranges broken by clusters of wood or metal objects—imposingly heavy presses and guillotines, down to the smallest gouges, for decorating leather.

Unfamiliar with the layout, the young woman found its size intimidating; it would be like looking for a needle in a haystack. Admittedly, the exposed areas could be ignored, but she was disconcerted by the huge number of cupboards and drawers, none of them apparently locked. Hopefully, they too could be overlooked as being too accessible for hiding places. . . . She pressed on. A second room, basically the same, was just as daunting. She was no detective; where did one start . . . ?

In the far corner she found a glass-fronted metal cabinet,

roughly the size and shape of a modern telephone box. From the dials and buttons of the control panel on one side, she guessed it was for drying paper; the bindery was famous for the conservation and restoration of early printed books and manuscripts, some of which might have the grime of centuries washed away before rebinding. The skills entailed were no doubt fascinating, but for the moment she had other matters on her mind.

The woman turned away . . . and then the penny dropped. The excitement was like an electric charge. What had the voice on the telephone said? Something about the necklace being concealed in *the last place anyone would look for "hot" property!* Until now she had not realized the significance of that remark. A refrigerator is what immediately sprang to mind, but since there was nothing resembling one in sight, this was surely the logical alternative.

Stepping back, she took a closer look at the controls to see if the panel was removable, or even if any of the buttons might unscrew completely, leaving a hole big enough for the flimsy piece of jewelry. But after that first flush of enthusiasm it was ominously clear that her assumption was not as inspired as she had imagined. She forced herself not to hurry, to work systematically, and made a mental note of details in case they should prove significant. On the panel there were measurements not only for temperature control but the regulation of humidity—presumably to prevent the paper from becoming baked. The temperature limit was one hundred degrees centigrade, and there was an automatic timer set to switch off after sixty minutes.

However, after a few moments' contemplation she sensed she was merely acquiring a fund of useless information, and transferred her attention to the interior, which, because of the area it covered, was more promising. It was possible, for a start, that the metal sheets did not fit as closely as it seemed from a distance.

Opening the door, she peered inside. The edges and corners were in shadow, and without knowing where the light switch was, she had to trace the metal edges with her fingertips. Near the bottom, in one corner, she encountered a small gap, worthy of further consideration, but it was so awkwardly situated as to be almost inaccessible and she had to get right inside, squatting on her haunches. So intent was she on examining her only lead that she was unaware of the door closing behind her. It was the sudden difference in air pressure that made her look around.

She pushed a languid arm against the door, but it seemed stuck, and for a split second she was disoriented. It was claustrophobic enough in the coffinlike cabinet even without the door shut. Stiffly she stood up so that she could lean her weight more evenly against the door; it refused to budge. Almost simultaneously she was conscious that in standing up her head was touching the ceiling. Instinctively she crouched a little, but the action made her more aware of her predicament.

A levelheaded person, she refused to panic. The worst that could happen would be the embarrassment of discovery when the staff returned. She glanced at her watch . . . in about forty minutes . . . if she did not die of boredom before then. As though ordinary trespass was not bad enough, how would she explain getting locked in the cabinet? *Sorry, I was looking for the toilet. . . .*

Despite the momentary flicker of amusement, she was conscious of perspiring. It was becoming stuffy in the cabinet, and her discomfort was not alleviated by a heavy cashmere sweater and tweed skirt. Even as she brushed the thought aside, she realized that it was the temperature more than the stuffiness that was bothering her, although it was difficult to determine if her imagination was to blame, exaggerating the normal buildup of body heat. But the rise was too marked for that; it was getting *hot*. . . .

At that point she was suddenly aware of the faint hum of a fan. She glanced over her shoulder and realized that hot air was blowing through a large grille in the cabinet's metal back. She took a deep breath to calm her nerves, but the air sucked into her windpipe felt like a clammy alien presence.

She was not the hysterical sort, but having grasped the fact that the rise in temperature was very real, the butterflies in her stomach took flight and there was a slight pain in her chest as they clogged her lungs, jostling for an escape route. In a somewhat detached manner it dawned on her that the closing of the door had somehow activated the drying mechanism. For a moment or two she resisted the panic, trying to convince herself that the buildup would be a gradual, gentle process, that anything too fierce would damage the irreplaceable paper that was normally dried in the cabinet.

Then she remembered that the gauge went up to one hundred degrees centigrade—the point at which her blood would boil—and her nerve cracked. She shouted for help at the top of her lungs, but from the muffled effect she realized that the sound was trapped every bit as effectively as her body. Then she began to scream and beat on the glass with hands and feet.

She was so preoccupied that it took at least a couple of minutes for the pain to travel up her limbs to her brain, but when it did, she was forced to stop. Her eyes focused on a symbol that indicated it was toughened Perspex she had been trying to smash. She was uncomfortably hot now, conscious of the perspiration drying on her skin the instant it emerged, and she knew she was in serious trouble. Whether or not it was the energy she had expended, her lungs began to labor, and at last she began to anticipate death almost rationally, wondering whether it would be through suffocation or heatstroke.

She forced herself to reject these morbid thoughts, knowing that the longer she could hang on, the greater the chance of one of the bindery staff returning from lunch and finding her. But it was becoming difficult to think coherently. The exposed flesh of her face and neck began to burn as though she had overdone a spell of sunbathing, and she pulled up her sweater to cover her head and face. It remained stiflingly hot, but the stinging sensation imperceptibly dulled. Her arms were still throbbing from her futile pummeling on the Perspex, but now she welcomed the distraction. She was feeling a little dizzy and leaned back weakly against the wall, only to pull herself away sharply as the heat from the hot metal penetrated her clothing.

The hot air attacking her seemed to be alive; it had the clinging substance of an evil entity. She knew it would help if she could smother it in some way, but the grille was too large an area to cover, even with her sweater, and that would have meant exposing her face and shoulders again.

The distressed brain was still sluggishly addressing the problem when she felt herself falling into a black hole. In fact, the descent was slowed by the proximity of the cabinet's sides, which acted as a brake, and she slid into an awkward heap on the floor, oblivious now of the hot metal that partially supported her. The face framed against the Perspex was like a beautiful death mask.

One of the drawbacks of living near the heart of a major city like London is the opportunity it affords friends and acquaintances to drop by unexpectedly for a nightcap after the theater, or an evening on the town. If pressed, I suppose I could probably recall an occasional welcome surprise—but, too often, these nocturnal "goodwill" visits coincided with a prior decision in favor of an early night.

Moving to Dorset, far from the rat race, I had been determined to capitalize on the chance to lead a life more suited to man's physiological needs; a decent night's sleep being an integral part of the healthy life in prospect. It was a pipe dream, of course. Despite the absence of distractions, and with none of the traditional excuses, I still found it impossible to get to bed before midnight—with the obligation of a naturalized country bumpkin to be up with the lark.

In all fairness, running an antiquarian and secondhand

bookshop in a busy little town like Ardley is not the nine-to-five doddle most people imagine. To sustain a healthy turnover, stock needs to be replenished on evenings and weekends; and since my standards are high, buying excursions mean regular visits to the neighboring counties, round-trips seldom less than fifty to sixty miles.

On the Tuesday it all began, I was feeling the pace after a particularly hectic couple of weeks; enough, that is, to make a conscious decision to squeeze in a full eight hours' sleep before my early morning run. Since for the same reasons I don't have time to read all I should, I took to bed the first volume of my latest prize acquisition, a first edition of *The Moonstone* by Wilkie Collins, published in 1868 in three volumes. Having picked up the novel for a mere £150 the previous day at a country-town auction the London dealers had somehow missed, I was in no hurry to sell; there would be no shortage of enthusiastic buyers. The value of *The Moonstone* lies not only in its "status"—it is the first full-length English detective novel of distinction—but especially in the rarity of the initial run with the misprint "treachesrouly" on page 129 of Volume Two. My purchase had the bonus of being in exceptionally fine condition for its age.

However, pleased though I was with my business acquisition, I was not going to lose the opportunity of reading it at last. Having enjoyed Collins' previous novel of suspense, *The Woman in White,* I wanted to decide for myself whether his insistence in classifying them as "serious" novels was anything more than the element of snobbishness toward detective fiction prevalent at the time. Within the first few pages I was left in no doubt of one thing: that Collins had a remarkable talent for creating characters every bit as real as those of his friend Dickens, and setting them in a haunting atmosphere that spilled from the pages of his books like ghostly images.

I was tired, yet my brain was stimulated by the story that unfolded, reawakening indefinable anxieties—the sense of unease that lurks in our subconscious. The shadows beyond the glow of my bedside lamp seemed to come alive so that my eyes scurried back to the reassuring brightness of the page. Earlier in the evening I might have embraced the eerie Gothic world threatening to invade my own, but gripped though I was by the narrative, my mind held back—conscious, perhaps, of the fast approaching witching hour of midnight. At least, that is the only explanation I can offer for hearing a noise downstairs and not reacting in the normal way. My heart leapt into my mouth, but the brain responded hesitantly, unable to distinguish the possible menace of reality from that of the book.

Looking back, such trepidation—making a mockery of my skills in the martial arts—may well have been a tribute to an almost forgotten Victorian author. All I know is that it took several minutes to appreciate that the noise I had heard had nothing to do with *The Moonstone*. Closing the book, I waited for confirmation that the suspicion had substance, but the eighteenth-century house was now as quiet as the grave.

Reasserting its authority, my brain demanded a logical explanation. The crime rate in Ardley was probably the envy of every reasonably-sized town in the South West, so burglary seemed only the remotest possibility. True, there were a handful of unemployed youngsters with an understandable ax to grind who might find books of greater interest than one of the local hardware stores or jewelers—but after a couple of preliminary skirmishes in the first few months of my arrival, I thought I had frightened them off.

There had been one scary attempt at arson, but that had been planned by a professional gang who had reason to fear the outcome of the investigation* I was conducting, and since then I had not been involved with what might be described as dangerous criminal elements.

There was open country at the back, and it was equally feasible that a fox or farm animal had found its way through the fence . . . except that an animal would still be moving about. When the list extended to the even fainter possibility that a book had fallen off a shelf in the stock area, I knew intuitively that I was clutching at straws. There was only one way to resolve the issue.

I slipped a pair of trousers over my pajamas and, wearing rubber-soled slippers, crept downstairs. Having taken the decision, I felt almost detached; fear returned whence it came, adrenaline awake but sluggish. Indeed, all I can remember is a mild irritation over the inconvenience that might be entailed if there was a burglar on the premises. I had no doubt about my ability to apprehend him, or them—but it would mean calling the police and then being saddled with the trappings of bureaucracy.

My stealthy approach took me through the main shop area—a sixth sense assuring me, even in darkness, that nothing had been disturbed. To reach a second bookroom accessible to customers I had to pass a display of antique pistols and swords decorating the wall above the high open fireplace, so attractive in winter—but I did not give them a moment's thought; striking an intruder with even the blunt edge of an old sword could land me in court on a manslaughter charge. In any case, I had the advantage of surprise. I knew every inch of the storeroom area and the

*A Cracking of Spines

outbuildings, and it was reasonable to assume that an intruder would not be armed. However, conscious of overconfidence, I grabbed an ornate, two-foot-long poker—part of the functional decor of the fireplace.

There was nothing to be seen; nor could I detect anyone through the glass door to the storage area, where the reserve stock is. It was so long since I had heard anything that I was beginning to suspect my imagination had overreacted, but suddenly there was the distinct sound of footsteps outside the back door. My adrenaline was kept in check by simple curiosity. The door was locked at night, yet two vertical glass panels in the upper section presented no obstacle to a determined burglar; but whoever it was outside must have been there for some time, presumably without making a serious effort to gain entry. Such apparent indecision seemed to rule out the seasoned criminal.

I silently unlocked the door and pulled it open suddenly—intent on scaring the living daylights out of the youngster I assumed would be standing there. But the figure facing me only a few feet away was an unexpected shock. The sinister gaunt frame draped in a long raincoat, collar pulled right up to hide the lower half of the face, might have stepped from the pages of *The Moonstone*. A dark, wide-brimmed felt hat deepened the shadows obscuring his face.

Fortunately, I still had the advantage of surprise—the stranger being even more disconcerted by my sudden appearance—and on hearing his sharp intake of breath, I dropped the poker and dived for his knees. He hit the path with a grunt of pain and shock, and before he could recover I had turned him on his face and was sitting astride his back. As his hat fell away, a handful of long hair in my left hand was all the leverage I needed to render him helpless, his face only inches from the concrete.

"All right," I exclaimed, endeavoring to keep the note of triumph from my voice. "This is private property. What were you doing?"

For a few seconds he struggled fruitlessly and then went limp. "I don't know. I wasn't thinking . . ." he eventually replied, the timbre of his voice strangely familiar.

Satisfied that he presented little further threat, I let go of his hair and pulled his right shoulder around so that we could make eye contact, but although my sight was becoming adjusted to the darkness, it was not sharp enough to bring his features into focus. Identification was further hampered by a heavy growth of beard.

"It's me," he intoned: "Mark Kingd—— Bill Ingham."

His hesitation might have been further grounds for suspicion, but for me the name was assurance enough that the stranger may have been in a state of confusion, but was certainly no burglar. I got up and pulled him to his feet; it was like lifting a dead weight.

"What was wrong with the front door?" I demanded.

"I didn't want to be seen."

Since the market square is a far cry from Piccadilly Circus, I was incredulous. "At this time of night? Come to think of it, if you're so shy, you could have saved yourself a journey and phoned."

"There wasn't time. I needed to see you. Can we go inside?"

I took my unexpected visitor into the office behind the shop where, in the light, I was able to see him clearly for the first time. He had changed since our last meeting a couple of years before, but I recognized him. Apart from the unfamiliar beard, he had lost about fifty pounds, so that the flesh had fallen away from the cheeks and he seemed all skin and bone. Coupled with a ghastly pallor, it made him look

ill, and I felt ashamed of my instinctive violence. We must
have been about the same age, but the man framed weakly
in the doorway might have passed for my father. Even the
piercing blue eyes with that remarkable luminescent quality
I remembered most of all were dulled by whatever it was
that had transformed him.

There is a self-contained little kitchen unit in the corner of
the room, and I filled the kettle. One did not need to be a
doctor to know that he was suffering from shock, and in the
absence of medical guidance, it seemed that hot, sweet tea
was the logical option. Meanwhile, having come all that
way to find me, he made no effort to talk; he might still
have been alone, lost in his thoughts. Even with the steam-
ing mug waved in front of his nose, Ingham remained preoccupied, although, when I sat, he followed my lead like an
automaton. Unable to relax, he perched on the edge of the
cushion.

"I need help," he began. "I didn't know where to turn
. . . and then I remembered Matthew Coll . . . a comfort-
ing face from the past. . . ."

I said nothing. Whether or not he was resorting to flat-
tery, we were strangers these days, and I could not believe
he did not have more intimate friends.

He seemed to read my thoughts. "I had to get out of
London—I'm wanted by the police. They will have checked
out my friends and acquaintances."

"Why are the police interested in you?"

"You know about my new life?"

I nodded. It dawned on me that he might be facing
charges of obtaining money under false pretenses; I didn't
really want to get involved.

"But you haven't heard anything today? Nothing on the
radio, or TV?"

"I don't have the box . . . no time. Normally I would have listened to the radio news, but tonight I went to bed early. As a matter of fact, you'll be interested in the book I took with me—a first edition of *The Moonstone*. I'll bring it down to show you. . . ."

I paused for a moment, half expecting his face to light up. The Ingham I knew had been a bibliophile, but he did not hear, or chose to ignore the invitation. Instead he produced a folded newspaper from the pocket of his raincoat and thrust it in my direction. "Tonight's *Standard* . . ."

I did not have to search for the story. My visitor had made the third lead on the London paper's front page.

MIRACLE GIRL MURDERED

BEAUTIFUL EX-CRIPPLE BATTERED TO DEATH

Jessica Seeley, twenty-three, whose sudden recovery from paralysis was hailed by medical authorities as "miraculous" only six months ago, was found dead at her home in Lexington Grove, St. John's Wood, last night. The body was discovered by her parents.

A postmortem is being conducted by Dr. John McPherson, the Home Office pathologist, but death is believed to have been caused by head injuries.

Police are treating the case as murder, describing the head wounds as "savage," and apparently inflicted by someone in a frenzy. They are investigating the theory that Jessica may have disturbed an intruder who then attacked her. She had not been sexually assaulted.

Detective Chief Inspector Paget, in charge of the murder squad, has announced that police wish to see several people connected with the girl and her parents, so that they may be eliminated from their inquiries. They are particularly anxious to interview Mr. Mark Kingdom, otherwise known as Bill Ingham, whose reputation as a faith healer was established overnight when he was given credit for restoring the power in Jessica Seeley's legs after conventional medical treatment over many years had failed. It is understood that Mr. Kingdom did not return to his London flat last night.

Murder! It was difficult to associate violence of any kind with the Bill Ingham I had known, but the person facing me now was a stranger. I felt no sympathy; indeed, it was no time for platitudes. "In what way did you think *I* could help?" I inquired.

He shrugged, avoiding my eyes, and, as though trying to escape further questions, got up and began to pace about the room.

I grabbed at a sleeve as he passed. Having been disturbed so unceremoniously, I was in no mood for guessing games. "Sit down," I commanded. "I don't suppose you've eaten all day. I'll cut some bread and cheese while you sort out your thoughts. . . ."

He shook his head. "I'm not hungry—just tired." As though on cue, he sat down again, this time leaning back in the armchair. He was obviously at the end of his tether, and it was difficult not to weaken my resolve to be firm.

I began again. "Why do the police want to question you?"

"They'll have assumed I killed her. . . ."

"It's hardly surprising, is it? Why did you take off if you had nothing to hide?"

"I was scared. You're the only person I know with any experience of these things. I thought you could tell me what to do."

I hesitated. It sounded simple enough, but Ingham's whole future might depend on that piece of off-the-cuff advice. "It's true you might find me a more sympathetic audience than the police, but at the end of the day you may *have* to face them," I pointed out. "I want to know something in confidence; you wouldn't have come a hundred miles without something on your conscience. The obvious question is: Did you kill her?"

He stared at me helplessly. "That's it. . . . I honestly don't know."

Bill Ingham and I had worked together on the *Daily Chronicle;* he was one of the reporters when I was personal assistant to Sir Stanley Drummond, the group's proprietor. We moved in different circles, but a mutual interest in old books made it more than a passing acquaintance, and when I left to become a bookseller, he was one of the few ex-colleagues who kept in touch for a time. The relationship ended when what had been a happy-go-lucky, down-to-earth journalist with no discernible religious convictions suddenly gave up a promising career—plus a wife and home that were the envy of many of his friends—to become a faith healer. It might have been accepted had he maintained a low profile, but it had happened in a blaze of publicity, supported with all the ballyhoo associated with Bible-thumping preachers. But his success had been meteoric, and there was even talk lately of his organization buying peak time on one of the new cable TV channels.

His closest friends alienated, Ingham—or Mark Kingdom, as he was now nationally known—had become increasingly isolated. I like to think I might have given his apparent sincerity as a healer the benefit of the doubt, but there was no longer any common ground between us.

Now he had reappeared and turned to me for help, I did not know where to begin. If I was tired, it was obvious that he was completely exhausted, yet I knew that if I went back to bed before getting a few explanations, I was in for a sleepless night too.

While he wolfed down the tea and cheese-and-tomato sandwiches I had forced on him, I put a camp bed in the spare room. We finished about the same time, and I was ready for a few answers. I needed to soak up enough of his story and background to enable me to make a rational judgment—enough, at least, to decide whether or not he should give himself up to the police first thing in the morning. The events of the past year or so were a lot to compress into a brief but coherent package, but his journalistic training came to the fore as he launched into his story.

"At the beginning it was all very low-key . . . the way it should have stayed—but that's another issue. It was the miracle—Jessica's cure—that changed everything. The first indication that people regarded me as someone special was when Jessica's mother kissed my hands. At first she had been suspicious, even hostile. Afterwards, she had all the unswerving faith of a convert, and although I'll remember the incident until the day I die, I was conscious all the time of a curious feeling of detachment, as though I was on the astral plane looking down. It seemed perfectly natural; after all, she had been witness to a miracle. . . ."

I wanted to break in and ask him about this so-called miracle. I had read about it in the newspapers at the time, but they had been typically sensational and I remember being skeptical. However, I did not want to interrupt his flow.

"No matter what the cynics said or even thought," he continued," *she* knew that, with God's help, I had cured her daughter. The doctors had failed. At last I was accepted for what I was. . . .

"In the months preceding Jessica's cure I must have changed gradually from the guy you knew on the *Chronicle,* but now my whole life-style had to be turned upside down. Because of the demands on my time, for example, there was the consideration of an alternative source of income. I was charging nothing, not even my expenses. People don't realize that. Admittedly there was only a handful of patients, all in the London area, but my opponents assumed they were being exploited. The only real problem had been my time, *finding* time almost every evening and weekend—time 'borrowed' from my wife and our friends.

"But when, as well as healing, the crusade Jessica's father had launched began to occupy my time during the day, my life had to be properly organized. They called in a specialist—a PR man called Doug Leighton—to 'stage-manage' the approach to new mass audiences. I suppose that's when it got out of hand; changed completely from the original intention."

"Why was that?"

He shrugged. "Professionalism. Well intentioned, but based on the assumption that what I was offering to the new audiences was no different to any commercial promotion. Without wishing to be blasphemous, can you imagine what they might do with Christ if he reappeared today? They may have been right—up to a point. The success I'd had so far was gained from talking intimately to people I had come to regard as friends in need of help, but it was obvious that to raise money we had to attract and retain large audiences. That meant a dramatic change in approach.

"Doug's background was show business, and I remember the analogy he used: He said it doesn't matter if you're promoting a soul singer or the Archbishop of Canterbury; you've got to grab 'em by the short hairs. I laughed at the time, but I realized he was right. They don't have to agree with you; they don't even have to like what you're saying—but get them to *listen*. They can't ignore your sincerity, he said. . . .

"The new campaign was launched at a press conference, and it was followed almost immediately by our first public meeting, which was the next milestone in my career. That was when I introduced the techniques that Doug had drummed into me. I wasn't proud of myself, but he proved it was the side of me that they wanted. People, especially the British, were shy, he said. No one likes to be the first to show his or her feelings. Doug got his experience at pop concerts, where he would pay a couple of kids to start the screaming; you know how quickly it spreads.

"So, my performance on the night—if I say so myself—was inspirational beyond my wildest dreams. It may not have been the original me speaking, but it was the Mark Kingdom they had come to see—someone with the fire of a Billy Graham and the gentle compassion of a healer anointed by God."

Although Ingham did an admirable job of editing, it was beginning to get light by the time the story was complete. The recounting of his experiences seemed to recharge his batteries, and before long his infectious enthusiasm pushed aside my own tiredness. The scene was set by his colorful re-creation of that important first meeting, but since much of it was not directly relevant to what I needed to form my opinion, I'll paraphrase the rest of his story.

It seems that the idea was to keep the audience in suspense

until Kingdom could be produced with a flourish. To set the mood, the guest of honor was Jessica Seeley, who must have been a PR man's dream. Having been groomed for the occasion, she not only looked fabulous but what she said, without prompting, rang with obvious sincerity and brought tears to many eyes. She described endless visits to hospitals, to specialists, even to priests . . . how everyone had shrugged sympathetic but helpless shoulders . . . everyone, that is, until Mark Kingdom came into her life. How he had treated her for months and not taken a penny.

The story was impressive. Jessica had been struck down by polio in her teens, and since the onset of paralysis the muscles had wasted, so that Kingdom had nothing upon which to work. She recalled how, even at their first meeting, she had recognized his powers, although it was not until he actually "laid on" his hands, some meetings later, that she actually felt the life force reentering her limbs.

Before the end of her story, the audience was putty in Kingdom's hands, although, inspired, it is not difficult to believe that he reached unscaled heights of oratory with his new-style address. As his passion reverberated around the massive hall, his eyes transfixed individuals as though it were to them alone he was speaking.

The Kingdom bandwagon was now well under way. After that triumphant start, people came to him from all over the country as he moved his operation from London to the major cities. But there were complications as Jessica's love for him imperceptibly descended to a more earthly plane. He found himself struggling to preserve a doctor-patient relationship that became strained and finally snapped . . . the prelude to disaster.

On the night Jessica was murdered, she had been pressuring him again . . . unable to comprehend why he did not return her love . . . until he felt as though his head would explode with the tension. Then he blacked out, and when he recovered she was dead.

Although I was no nearer knowing who had killed Jessica Seeley—and to what extent Ingham was himself involved— I was impressed by his sincerity. It didn't matter at this stage whether the so-called power channeled through his hands by God was genuine or imagined. What concerned me was the sight of a former friend, harried from pillar to post until his nerve had cracked and he was unable to face the reality of a possible murder charge. He deserved, at least, the chance to rest, to collect his thoughts, and to decide on a course of action away from the pressures of his former life. I told him he could stay . . . at least for a few days.

Ingham (I could not bring myself to call him by his adopted name) said nothing, but the relief in his face was expressive enough, and I began to wonder if I could not do more to help. I was in possession of information to which the police had not yet had access, so I already had a head start. . . .

I stopped the tempting train of thought. I had a bookshop to run. The "action" was in London, and I could not afford to close for the duration. It was not just a question of the money; the shop provided a service—no idle boast, because the town of Ardley represented only a part of our trade, customers being spread over a hundred-mile radius of the town.

My introspection was interrupted by Ingham's heavy sigh at the beautiful landscape, which was becoming clearer by the minute from the back window. On a bright day it is possible to take in sixty miles of coastline. "With views like this, how do you do any work?" he said, as though thinking aloud and not expecting an answer. "For the past year

I've been cut off—cocooned . . . trapped in personal rela-
tionships by people who didn't expect me to have any outside interest. If only I'd been given a day off a week, even
the Sabbath that God commanded, to get away from people. I might never—" He broke off. "Why am I complain-
ing? At least, I've got my health . . . a damned sight more
than those who come to depend on me."

My mind was practically made up; it was time someone
did something to help *him* for a change. "I've got a good
friend, a retired bookseller called Charles Appleton, who
comes in sometimes to help out. For Charlie it's a labor of
love, although it's quite a journey. What are your relations
with Drummond?"

He seemed confused by the break in my train of thought.
"Drummond?"

"Sir Stanley. Our former boss. The Godfather."

He smiled at the title, and shrugged. "I never got as far as
the top floor. I was a reporter, not a feature writer. I don't
suppose he was sad to see me leave. The *Chronicle* was
pretty embarrassed by the whole business."

"There must have been much sucking of the royal breath,
and the raising of eyes to heaven," I said. "The man has no
interest in life outside the papers, but that could be to your
advantage. If I can persuade him that the *Chronicle* will get
an eventual exclusive on Jessica's murder—your story, in
the first person, if necessary—then subsidizing Charlie's
wages here for a week or so is no more hardship than dipping into petty cash. It would save me having to find the
money."

Ingham pulled a face. "I'd like to fund you myself, but
the only person with access to my money is Mr. Seeley,
Jessica's father. He's a fine man, but in the circumstances

. . . I can't say I'm keen on going to the *Chronicle* . . . can
you imagine what a field day they'll have. . . ?"

"You, of all people, should know that there has to be a
story for someone. At least with an exclusive, you'd have
some measure of control. And if we can prove your innocence, the *Chronicle* would have a vested interest in being
sympathetic—one of their 'old boys,' and all that. . . ."

Having made the decision, I let Ingham get some sleep,
but my own bed looked cold and uninviting and I decided
the time could be better occupied preparing for the task
ahead. In any case, trying to grab a couple of hours with my
head buzzing with ideas was scarcely better than no sleep at
all, and I would feel terrible on waking. Instead, I took a
warm bath followed by a cold shower and twelve minutes
of Canadian Air Force exercises in place of the morning run.
Shaved, dressed, and breakfasted, I felt a new man.

Sir Stanley Drummond was one of those tycoons who
was at his desk by seven-thirty every morning, grumbling
at the cost of paying exorbitant wages—seldom more than
the union minimum—for "part-time" staff. The paper was
ostensibly a twenty-four-hour-day operation, but it was not
unknown for Sir Stanley to be taking calls before the
switchboard was fully operational in the morning. Indeed, I
was not surprised to get straight through to him.

When I worked for the *Chronicle,* the relationship had
been amiable enough. In an unguarded moment he professed to liking me, but that did not stop him from com-
plaining bitterly of "disloyalty" when I announced my
decision to leave. My intuition about his reaction to helping
us now was borne out. He cared nothing for Ingham, the
reporter who had "betrayed" his colleagues, or me, whom
he regarded as an eccentric for choosing to sell books and

live in Dorset. But at the prospect of a major story exclusive to the *Chronicle,* he was prepared to listen, albeit with a degree of cynicism. "The man is round the twist," he insisted. "I trust you've got him in a safe place. As soon as the police get their hands on him, he'll be charged, and that means no story at all until the trial—which is useless to us."

I controlled my irritation at his single-mindedness. "If Ingham is a murderer, then there isn't much of a story, anyway . . . at least, not one you can print. I should have thought the attraction was the prospect of the *Chronicle* turning up the real killer. That'll give you two stories—the murder, which is juicy enough, and the untold story of Mark Kingdom, the miracle man almost martyred but saved at the eleventh hour by another miracle. . . ."

"I still say he's missing a few marbles. What makes you think he's innocent?"

In other circumstances I might have resorted to bluff, but since I was asking him to fund the operation, my conscience rebelled. "It's not so much what I think as giving him a fair deal. I need about a week or so to make the necessary inquiries before we have to worry about him giving himself up. The point is I've already got a head start on the police."

"And you want the *Chronicle* to fork out for you to follow up some unsubstantiated whim of yours that he's innocent. . . ?"

I saw red. "Forget it. I wasn't asking for charity. We'll go it alone; Ingham can pay me back when he sells his story to the highest bidder. . . ."

Drummond snorted. "If that's the way you repay my friendship . . ."

But I had already put the phone down.

3

The only "independent" information I had about Jessica Seeley's death was what I had read in *The Standard,* which was presumably based on the bare bones issued by Scotland Yard. Reading between the lines, it seemed that little weight had been given to the theory of Jessica's disturbing an intruder because the police already had a suspect. There was no indication of the discovery of material evidence of any sort, so if the police were in possession of a murder weapon complete with Ingham's fingerprints, I was wasting my time.

I had no contacts in the Metropolitan Police, and no prospect of meeting Chief Inspector Paget, but I did have a relationship of sorts with Ardley CID through Detective Inspector Murdoch, who had become a personal friend, despite the number of times we had crossed swords. Unlike any policeman of my acquaintance, Jamie Murdoch was almost a caricature of a country gentleman, although I suspect one of the reasons I had a soft spot for him was that he reminded me of my schooldays and a particular geography master who had left his heart in the Himalayas, capturing our youthful imaginations with romantic tales of the North-West Frontier. Murdoch had the same twinkling blue eyes overhung with shaggy sun-bleached eyebrows. When he smiled, which was frequently, the eyes practically disappeared under that heavy blond thatch. He was a tall, craggy individual, a tower of strength to anyone in need of his help, but dangerous to cross. Our friendship had begun uneasily with a basis of mutual respect and developed as we both mellowed and tried to meet the other halfway.

The line between capitalizing on one's friendship and abusing it is a fine one. Murdoch went by the book, and I would not normally ask him about police inquiries, but a man's life might be at stake and I had to risk upsetting him because I had no illusions about the CID of any metropolis. It would not surprise me if Ingham were arrested on circumstantial evidence alone; city police did not have the time to be as thorough as the job demanded. If that happened, the chances then of convincing them that he might be innocent were even more remote. A delicate issue, especially as I was concealing a wanted man in my home; I had to resist the temptation to hide behind a phone call.

In fact, I paid him a visit at breakfast time, intent on catching him away from the formality of his office. "Morrrning, Murrrdoch," I announced, rolling my r's in a wild exaggeration of his faintest Scots burr. "Sorry to call before you're dressed, but it was urgent."

That, too, was a calculated insult because he looked as immaculate as ever; the only concession to the early hour and the privacy of his home being the absence of a jacket.

Whatever the circumstances, he had a knack for making me feel untidy.

An instinctive smile of welcome was replaced by an expression of concern. "You're after something?" he speculated.

His wife, Maureen, called from the kitchen. "If it's the milkman, I need an extra pint. . . ."

"It's not the milkman," he retorted. "It's trouble."

As she came bustling through to the front door, her anxious expression was replaced by a smile of relief on recognizing me. A tall, well-groomed woman of middle age with a pretty face and happy personality, Maureen Murdoch ran half a dozen charity committees in the town and was universally liked. "Why is Matt standing there like a door-to-door salesman?" she chided her husband.

Murdoch led the way in, muttering under his breath about the naïveté of women. "He's no different to a salesman; whenever this man phones or calls at the station, he's after something," he told her. "Don't imagine this is a social visit. . . ."

"Social visit? You don't know what that means. When is the last time you *invited* me round?"

"Last week," came the triumphant retort.

Since I could not argue with a fact, I responded to Maureen's invitation to sit at the table and helped myself to some cornflakes; it seemed ages since I had had my own breakfast. "If you insist that I had to have a reason for calling round . . ."

Murdoch snickered and appealed to his wife for support. "You think that because this guy has the ability to look you in the eye when he speaks, he's telling the truth. . . ."

"Are you saying I lie to you?"

"Perhaps you don't lie," he conceded. "But you tell me only as much as you think I ought to know."

I laughed. "Because you're always so busy; I don't like to burden you with detail."

Maureen took my side. "I don't know why you're so indignant, Jamie Murdoch—you only tell me what you think I ought to know. . . ."

"What I think will *interest* you," he corrected.

"Exactly," I echoed. "What would you say if I admitted it was Maureen I came to see? You should have been at work by now."

Murdoch raised an eyebrow. "That I *can* believe. My wife is an attractive woman."

She poked me in the ribs. "Keep it up—he's never said that before." She kissed her husband. "Thank you, darling. But exciting though it sounds, we've both seen Laura, and Matt would have to be crazy to look at another woman."

I winced at the accuracy of her remark. Laura Cottingham and I had an "understanding" that was complicated by the fact that she lived in London, and as a director of a major advertising agency her annual income was probably twice that of mine. Laura was a beautiful woman, highly intelligent and with a bubbling personality; in fact, she could not be faulted, except perhaps in that she was prepared to put up with my shortcomings. People have assumed that I take advantage of the relationship, but it could be said that I am too considerate to ask her to give up the advantage of her current life-style to settle down with me in Ardley.

I was suddenly aware that Maureen had left us together and that Murdoch, putting on his jacket, was preparing to leave, so I quickly came to the point. "I should have known you could read me like a book," I simpered. "It *is* you I wanted to see. I need some information. . . ."

He said nothing, but the corners of his mouth turned up as he studied me under those enormous eyebrows.

"Have you heard yet about the so-called miracle girl who has been found dead in London?"

He nodded. "A few lines in the morning paper."

"Do you know the man in charge of police inquiries?"

"I don't think so—at least, the name didn't ring a bell. . . ."

"Detective Chief Inspector Paget."

"If that's what you read . . ."

"That was the name in the paper."

Murdoch shrugged. "You know what I think of the media's unconcern for accuracy. What is it to you?"

"Just curious."

Murdoch laughed.

"This faith healer they want to interview—Mark Kingdom. I used to know him. I wouldn't have thought he was a murderer. . . ."

Murdoch was not fooled by my air of detachment. "You know your friends better than me. I'm hardly in a position to pass judgment on half a dozen lines of dubious authenticity in a morning newspaper."

"It was the accuracy or otherwise of the report that disturbed me. These things can be phrased in such a way as to give the impression the police have an open-and-shut case. . . ."

"Such as what?"

". . . 'Police wish to interview So-and-So, so that he can be eliminated from their inquiries. . . .'"

"Nothing wrong with that," Murdoch remarked blandly. "If he's got nothing to hide, he *will* be eliminated from their inquiries. I don't know what story he's fed you, but you would be wise to be very circumspect in how you react. . . ."

I deflected his inspired shot in the dark. "I've less con-

fidence than you in the diligence of the Met. Whether or not
it's the problem of time—I know how overworked they
are—they're obsessed with quick answers . . . if circumstantial evidence is enough, why look any further? There are
plenty of other cases to be getting on with. . . ."

Surprisingly Murdoch did not attempt to defend his colleagues in London. "You may have a point. In an ideal
world, there would be less margin for error, but even so we
don't make many mistakes. Statistics show that we don't
have to look very far for our murderers; nine times out of
ten they come from the victim's immediate circle. Your objection to neat and tidy solutions is not a rational one because I can assure you that's what they usually are . . .
conforming to one pattern or another."

"And what about those which don't conform?"

He inclined his head to concede the point. "What did you
have in mind?"   .

I hesitated. I would have liked to match my friend's professionalism, but going to bat on a hunch was beginning to
seem naïve. "Nothing specific. But in my judgment Bill
Ingham—that was his name when I knew him on the *Daily
Chronicle*—is no murderer. I'm tempted to make a few inquiries for old times' sake—but, obviously, there's no point
in wasting my time if this man Paget has irrefutable evidence. What I need to know is how the girl actually died,
and what the line of inquiry is. . . ."

Murdoch sighed. "You know what I think about interference from outsiders."

"Hardly interfering. I agree I haven't always kept out of
your hair, but this is different. I've no vested interest this
time . . . other than the truth."

"Even talking to witnesses constitutes interference. . . ."

"Why?"

"I'm late," he announced, the discussion at an end.

"All I had in mind was to speak to Kingdom's friends—build up a picture of his state of mind. If he's guilty, then what I discover can't concern the prosecution, and may be of some value to his defense, which you would not begrudge, surely. . . ?"

"All right. I'll make a few calls and contact you later, after which perhaps you'll let the matter drop. But if you do proceed, I'll need your word as a friend you'll behave yourself. If I hear of you getting in Paget's hair, I won't attempt to protect you."

Laura Cottingham and I spoke on the phone fairly frequently, but we saw each other only when I had occasion to go to London for an auction, or when she came to Ardley for a long weekend. Murdoch's news that the CID had little to go on, and that suspicion of Mark Kingdom had been fired only by his inexplicable disappearance, provided another opportunity to see her.

People seldom understood the relationship. Laura and I were close friends, but because we chose for the moment to lead separate lives, there had to be a large measure of flexibility in the arrangement. I had to accept, for example, that over the first three evenings of the week or so I expected to spend in town, she had business or social engagements. Whether any of the men who were part of this life ever stayed the night, I never asked; it had to be enough in the circumstances that our relationship always took precedent. If I was staying at her flat and she had a prior engagement I would not allow her to break, she would return with her escort, introduce us, and after a nightcap send him on his way. Marriage might have been preferable, but at what cost?

Laura's home was a two-bedroom flat on the fifth floor of a luxury block at the back of Marble Arch, for which the service fee—the sort that represented a change of fresh flowers in the lobby every day—was as much as many people pay for their mortgage repayments. Only someone in her high income bracket could afford that sort of place, and while I had no reason to be ashamed of the beautiful Queen Anne building that housed my home and shop, the two were of different worlds. It seemed sensible to hang on to both.

I had decided that Ingham was entitled to underwrite the cost of my inquiries because one way or another he would not be short of money. If Sir Stanley Drummond refused to grasp the olive branch, then the rest of Fleet Street would come begging for the chance of an exclusive about Ingham's relationship with the dead girl. I would trust Charlie Appleton with my life, so when he arrived to take over the shop, I had no hesitation about revealing Ingham's true identity. There was little chance of his being recognized in this unfamiliar setting, so, providing he kept a low profile, he could use the time to recharge his batteries, do some reading, and even help Charlie with some cataloging. By the time I left, he was already looking relaxed, and more like the man I had once known.

I found Drummond subdued, even contrite by his standards, and it was not difficult to formalize the arrangement. Another advantage to me was that by representing the *Chronicle* group, I could, within reason, call on other enormous resources; it also gave me a degree of authority that might impress people who would not feel inclined to talk frankly with a small-country-town bookseller.

My plan was simple: to see everyone connected with Mark Kingdom who might be aware of his relationship with the dead girl. Her parents were an obvious starting point, but I dreaded the prospect. Apart from the moral issue, Mr. Seeley had found the body and was therefore a principal witness while Bill Ingham could yet find himself in the dock. By any standards, probing at such recently opened wounds was a daunting proposition and would have to wait until I was a little surer of my ground. And since Ingham was living apart from his wife, who was now modeling in Paris, she too would have to wait. My priority was Douglas Leighton, who had been the faith healer's campaign manager, and who must have been closer to him than anyone in recent months.

The *Chronicle* news-desk team were an invaluable source of information, and it was through them that I obtained Leighton's telephone number, made contact, and arranged a lunch date at the Press Club, membership of which I had retained—one of my few concessions to the old life. I had the impression Leighton accepted the invitation only because, as a publicist, he did want to cross swords with the *Daily Chronicle,* and because it was always useful to be seen around the Press Club. He was obviously known, because he arrived early and when I turned up at the correct time, it was the barman who introduced us. Leighton had a large Scotch in his hand, and I guessed from his complexion that he liked alcohol.

We were about the same height, but I reckoned he was at least twenty pounds overweight. He might once have been an athlete; he moved with a certain style and grace. In his early thirties, he looked like a man popular with both sexes: pleasant features craggy and scarred as a boxer's, expressive, warm blue eyes, and even white teeth that he displayed at every opportunity. When he was not smiling, the small mouth looked weak—not that I normally pay much attention to this sort of instant character assassination; some of the toughest men in my experience had looked effeminate and often were. The overall picture was likable, and I felt sufficiently at ease to inquire whether my original impression about his reluctance to meet was justified.

"I really don't want to talk about Mark Kingdom," he confirmed in a rich baritone. "After giving him several months of my life, I suddenly find myself out of work and, it seems, in rather bad odor. Furthermore, I'm stony broke. All I've got to sell is the Mark Kingdom story, and I've been negotiating very promisingly with the *Sunday Record*. I can't allow anything to prejudice that deal."

I sympathized, but pointed out that I was not representing the *Chronicle* as a journalist. But he knew the newspaper business better than I, and his smile registered disbelief. "Since I know more about the background to the murder than anyone, apart from Kingdom—perhaps even more, in some respects—my story in the *Record* would be in direct competition with any other exclusive story carried by your paper, so I have to protect my interest," he said.

Somewhat naïvely I asked if we could come to some financial arrangement and he seemed mildly shocked, explaining that his reticence was simply a question of prior loyalty to the *Record*. We remained at the bar, talking around the subject, when on his fourth double Scotch he suddenly mellowed and agreed to accept my written undertaking not to use any of the information gained from our discussion in any *Chronicle* editorial feature, and not to take notes during the interview. I tore out a page of my notebook and solemnly scrawled the necessary wording. I didn't know whether the promise was binding by legal standards, but he seemed to be happy. The deal was sealed with another

drink, although I merely ordered a fresh tonic water to top
up my second gin, and we went to lunch.

After we had ordered, I told him that I needed to hear an
account of his relationship with Kingdom in some sort of
chronological order, but wanted first to get his reaction to
the disappearance. He shrugged. "It's as big a mystery to
me as anyone—not that I expect you to believe that. . . ."

"Why not?" I protested. "I wouldn't have put the question if I didn't think you were truthful."

Whatever Leighton's preoccupation with self-preservation—and who could blame him?—he apparently had no
intention of painting Kingdom in a bad light. He made no
secret of the fact that he admired his client and believed him
to be gifted with mystical powers. Yet, faced with the circumstantial evidence of Jessica's death and the disappearance, he was at a loss to suggest an explanation. "In
normal circumstances, the Mark Kingdom I knew was incapable of murder," he said, "but recently he had been
plagued with these strange visions. . . ."

"You mean hallucinations?"

He studied me with barely concealed impatience. "That
depends on whether you're a skeptic, or you have an ax to
grind. Joan of Arc was burned at the stake because she insisted that God talked to her in visions. No one really *cared*
if what she said had any element of truth. It was politically
expedient to make an example of her. . . ."

"There are no political implications here," I argued. "But
if there is a difference between the two interpretations, his
defense counsel would need to know."

"If and when he turns up, you'll have to ask him," suggested Leighton calmly, "and then make your own judgment. I happen to believe they were real, even though Bill
had his doubts. He was always the last to accept what has

been obvious to others. It's not just false modesty; it just took a lot more to convince him."

I had to respect Leighton's judgment, but as a salesman, was he a sucker for his own sales talk? I reassured him, telling him we were really on the same side, but that I could not afford to rely on instinct. What effect, I asked, would "visions" or "messages" have had on his relationship with the girl, and could he have killed her when in that state?

"You'll have to ask someone else," he replied. "I admit to being prejudiced in his favor. The evidence is entirely circumstantial—she died from a crushed skull, and the murder weapon was presumably a silver candlestick, but that's all we really know. Jessica was just learning to walk again and was unsteady when she was tired—she could have fallen over and banged her head. You've got to remember that if she lost her balance, she would have gone over like a dead weight. . . ."

I shook my head. "There was blood and hair on the candlestick . . . somebody used it to hit her."

He shrugged. "I'm scared he may be dead. If he's not, I wonder whether there might be something buried in his subconscious . . . something that could be reached under hypnosis or drugs. . . ."

I did not tell him I had seen Ingham, promising to look into the matter, before bringing the conversation back to the beginning of their relationship. During the rest of the meal he related his side of the story. . . .

I was close to Bill [Leighton began]. Closer than anyone, once he realized I knew what I was talking about and had his interests at heart. In the very early days, there were several people—friends of Mr. Seeley—trying to manage his affairs, and thinking they knew all the answers simply because they were moderately successful in the City, or in business. They meant well, I suppose, but it was a question of "too many cooks," and gradually we persuaded them to leave all the organization and promotion to me.

My problem for some time was trying to define a saleable program, because Bill was highly cautious of anything that had selling undertones. You know the attitude. "People must accept me for what I am," and all that rubbish, and I had to explain over and over again that we were in effect trying to market a product—a package called Mark King-dom—and promotion was an integral part of that market-ing operation. You can have the best product in the world, but if nobody knows about it . . .

It took a long time for that message to sink in, but when it did, there was an overnight transformation.

The first hurdle was the press conference, and Bill and I compromised—using the soft-sell style of delivery he fa-vored, but backing it up with chapter and verse on every aspect of faith healing and religion that could possibly be anticipated. We rehearsed a permutation of questions and answers for hours, and when the test came, he passed with flying colors. The coverage was not spectacular, but we had already had a wadge of sensationalism, so the rather muted aftermath came almost like an endorsement of his respect-ability from the press.

I thought he'd share my delight, but for some reason Bill was upset on the day after the press conference. I don't know whether it was seeing many of his old friends again and still not being really one hundred percent certain he was cut out for faith healing, or whether it was a normal reac-tion following such a major test. But he was depressed and withdrawn when I picked him up next morning, so I tried to take him out of himself by going to look at the venue for our first public meeting—you probably know it—the Wagner Memorial Hall in Marylebone. It's not exactly a palace, but we had to feel our way at that stage; couldn't go for anything grander until we knew whether we could attract a following.

His spirits must have sunk even lower when we first looked around because it's pretty spartan, with a wood block and stone floor and uniform rows of folding chairs. It's ideal for boxing and wrestling shows, where people get too excited to notice the surroundings, but when you're a sensitive individual contemplating your first confrontation with an audience . . . it must have been a bit off-putting.

But as usual, he responded to common sense, and I explained that we would have enough critics without throwing our limited funds around on trimmings and trappings. The Café Royal might sound very nice, but it was *people* who mattered . . . people who could warm the barest hall. In any case, we could not go for anything as impressive as Wembley Stadium until we knew in practice we could draw more than a few hundred or so.

We were living from hand to mouth—Bill on money in lieu of notice from the *Chronicle,* and me on a small handout from the funds Mr. Seeley and his associates had put up. Perhaps a lot in their eyes—all of them living in the past— but by present-day standards it was ridiculous. The hours I was putting in—not only as a one-man "think tank," but as head cook and bottle washer, merited *ten* times the fee. I looked after everything, literature, posters, getting blokes from the local labor exchange to act as stewards—everything, while Bill got on with his speech and kept his patients happy. Apart from Jessica and Ben Lawton, who got all the publicity, he'd had Emily Miles, a crippled widow in her sixties, and a lad in his teens, whose parents, I've just heard, have discreetly removed him since the latest drama.

Bill's only link with the past was Norah Peters, who took him in after the breakup of his marriage. She is manager of the bindery at the National Library in South Kensington. Come to think of it, I'm surprised the police—if they knew about the affair—haven't taken a look at her flat. If he's hiding anywhere, that's the place I'd try. I don't know whether the relationship was a good or bad thing, because although she absolutely dotes on him, inevitably she magnified the gulf between his former self and Mark Kingdom. During the day he was a faith healer, but when he went back to her most nights, the doubts and confusion must have started all over again.

Anyway, we had high hopes for the Wagner Memorial Hall. There was seating for about three hundred and fifty, and standing room—with a bit of a squeeze—for another hundred or so. I estimated that with the correct use of the collection boxes, an attendance three-quarters capacity would probably cover the cost of hire and advance publicity; while anything over that number would show a profit—which was something we'd ruled out at this stage. In the very unlikely event of an overcapacity crowd, we'd have to apologize for the inconvenience and rub our hands all the way to the bank. The publicity value would also be enormous.

If that sounds cold-blooded, I'm giving the wrong impression because I put more sweat—time and effort—into that crummy little operation than if I'd been producing a star-studded million-dollar charity show—not because I was being paid (I've told you what that was worth) but because I believed in Bill and wanted to play a part in communicating that belief to others. So there was a fair bit of inspiration and talent going for us that night.

We had a final briefing in Bill's flat at midday, so that everyone knew exactly what was expected of him. I'd reckoned that unlike a blasé West End theater audience, they would all be in their seats in good time, so we could start bang on the dot of eight. The stage was kept completely empty until that point, when Mr. Seeley emerged, introducing himself, and explaining how and why the scheme was launched. Then, as their anticipation mounted, he introduced Bill's first three patients, all of whom had benefited in some degree from his healing.

I took a chance on using someone inexperienced like Mr. Seeley as chairman on a public platform, but I realized that his sincerity would be a major factor with this sort of audience. In any case, I didn't want anyone too smooth who might have shown up any shortcomings in Bill's public manner—not that I need have worried. He was fantastic, better than my wildest expectations. And that goes for Jessica too. She was a beautiful kid. A bit dowdy and withdrawn—which was obviously something to do with her illness—but I'd given her advice on makeup and the right hairstyle, and she turned up trumps. The legs were obviously her only drawback, so we covered them as glamorously as possible in black velvet jeans, and above them in what was her own choice—a simple white or silver Lurex evening smock with three-quarter-length sleeves. She was so stunning, I made some crack about diverting the audience from the main attraction, but we were really all delighted.

Old Ben was late—despite the fact that we had sent a car for him—but Mrs. Miles was just right, and we decided to start. We kept trying to reach Ben by phone, but the line was persistently engaged, so we didn't get the news of his death—and then in the worst possible manner—until the middle of the meeting. You may have heard what happened

or seen something in the cuttings . . . it was a close thing.
It's no joke when someone—in this case it was Ben's son—
bursts in and calls you every name under the sun, from fake
to murderer! If I say so myself, it was only my experience
that got us off the hook. No matter how well one prepares
for such eventualities, there is always something it's impossible to guard against. It's that sort of long-shot bomb drop-
ping right in your lap that separates the men from the
boys—or, in this context, the pro from the amateurs. I'd
rather it hadn't happened, of course, but in the event Bill
came out of the mire smelling like roses, although, as usual,
it seemed to spark off all his original doubts.

It was in the midst of that depression that the visions
started. They happened on average about once a week . . .
and I regarded each one as a communicaton from God. Bill
picked up the most fantastic messages in a kaleidoscope of
color images. I can only scratch at the surface if I try to
explain or describe them, because he was invariably alone at
the time; you would have to ask him. All I know is that
they had a pretty powerful impact and usually left him exhausted, and sometimes depressed again at the responsibility
on his shoulders. As far as Mr. Seeley and the others were
concerned, it was merely further proof, if it was needed, of
his powers.

When our second meeting went off well, we tried our
hand in Birmingham, and partly because of the advance
publicity I'd fixed with the local press, we had a full house.
The collection was so encouraging that we had a problem
deciding whether to charge for admission next time, or rely
again on the audience's generosity. We didn't have time to
reach a decision because, as you know, a few days later
Jessica's death upset the apple cart. I reckon that with my
drive and enterprise, and eventually cable TV, we would

have been taking really big money within a couple of years. It's a tragedy that Bill will probably never see the fame and success he deserves because, even if he's alive and even if he is tried and acquitted, we'll never persuade him to pick up where he left off. Mark Kingdom has been lost to the world.

Leighton was practically crying in his Scotch by the time he had completed his version of the story of Kingdom the Healer, and I began to wonder how much the combination of emotion and drink had affected his memory. He obviously knew and cared little about the real Ingham, despite the fact that he referred to him as Bill, but surely what I wanted was a dispassionate assessment? It was possible that the man I had known had changed beyond recognition.

I went back to the *Chronicle*'s library to go through the cuttings more thoroughly, but they did not help. I needed to speak to someone completely impartial, who would help me to step back and reassess the perspective I had of the case. I was suddenly impatient to see Laura. It would be late before she returned, but we had the advantage of being able to talk in bed.

In making a point about Laura Cottingham's intelligence I run the risk of being labeled "chauvinist"; it should be apparent that no one could achieve such success in a tough, competitive world like advertising without outstanding ability. My reason for bringing it up at all is that she uses her colorful looks and personality as a distraction, in the same way as a boxer feints to keep an opponent off-balance. Laura saw to it that only a few friends and colleagues were aware of her full potential.

As I had anticipated, she shared my fascination for Ingham's involvement in the life and death of Jessica Seeley. Admittedly, she had a vested interest in motivations and behavior patterns, but what really captured her imagination was the reaction of the individual to *ab*normal influences; how he or she responds to overwhelming pressures. She was somewhat cynical, however, about Ingham's alleged powers, and especially the reverent attitude of associates like Doug Leighton.

"How can you be so po-faced about all that bilge?" she said.

"I only believe what is on record. Mark Kingdom cured a cripple; that isn't disputed. I don't claim to know how. If he reckons it was the power of God, who am I to call him a liar?"

Her expression was wide-eyed. "Since when did *you* believe in God?"

"I didn't say I believed anything—I'm trying to keep an open mind. A person's views are formed from personal experience, and because you and I haven't had the sort of messages he talks about doesn't mean we should call him a fraud. If there *is* a God, it isn't so farfetched to accept that he would probably work through ostensibly ordinary men and women. A number of so-called prophets didn't recognize their calling until adulthood; Muhammad is a good example."

"The danger is that you've set out on a presumption that he has special powers—which means that all the so-called evidence you establish from now on has to fit that preconception."

"Not true. My first appointment tomorrow is with George Kester, the columnist. They were close friends before Ingham became a healer. I'm not going to find him as wide-eyed as Leighton. He's hardheaded enough to make even you seem like a starry-eyed romantic."

I knew Kester by reputation. He had run the paper's gossip column for the past fifteen years, since his early twenties—very young by Fleet Street standards. It was generally considered that his impressive talent was out of proportion to the content of popular papers like the *Chronicle,* but this applied to several of its name writers because, for some indefinable reason, the paper managed to instill a strong loyalty among the editorial staff.

Kester was a thickset, prematurely bald man who conformed to the layman's image of a newspaper columnist, and it only needed the addition of a green eyeshade to transform him into a caricature. He was never without a cigarette, although he generally only smoked about half and filled his ashtray with a mountain of giant stubs; but a trail of tobacco smoke would constantly find its way from ashtray, nicotine-stained fingers, or the corner of his mouth into his eyes, so that he seemed to have a perpetual squint. His mouth constantly grimaced with the taste of whiskey, which he appeared to use more as a mouthwash than a drink, because his consumption of alcohol was not unduly high, and he was never drunk.

I met him in the tiny goldfish bowl of an office that distinguished name writers from the rest of the editorial team. He was courteous enough, although I couldn't tell whether the sour expression mirrored his mood or his opinion of me and the task I had undertaken, or was due to the sip of whiskey he had just sampled. There was no other glass in evidence and he offered me a plastic beaker, but it looked a little dusty. He was amused by my apparent fastidiousness, but I wasn't there to impress Kester.

I explained that I wanted to get different perspectives on Ingham's behavior in the past year, and gave him a potted version of the PR man's story, without going into detail or offering an opinion. He listened with genuine interest, displaying none of the bitterness I had half expected. When he offered no comment, I asked that question.

"I got the impression you were once very close," I said, "but you turned against him. Why was that?"

He screwed up his eyes, but I couldn't tell whether the cigarette smoke was making them sting or whether he found the memory painful. When he eventually replied, the tone was one of surprise. "He was a delightful fellow," he conceded. "Could even be quite amusing. . . . Had a flair for impersonating celebrities; you know, Jimmy Cagney and Cary Grant . . . even females. The humor vanished when he graduated to doing God; that wasn't funny at all!"

"That doesn't answer my question," I pointed out. "True friendship ought to make allowances for these things; that is, if you were close enough."

"Sure, we were close, but what do you do when you find your best friend is beating his wife and kids?"

"You don't mean that literally?" I asked.

He ignored the question. "There is a limit to how much you can make allowances for other people's indiscretions. They say we're only human, and that's so bloody right. We're all of us full of imperfections. But this wasn't a question of a guy falling down a couple of times. . . . It began with a calculated decision, against strong opposition from those who loved him, and continued with a slow and gradual change of personality, so that he wasn't the same guy anymore. Bill Ingham was my friend and might still be, if he existed. The person facing a murder charge is Mark Kingdom—not the man I knew."

"I can understand that," I conceded, "but how can you be so sure that the Bill Ingham you knew is not still there, trying to get out?"

His expression was cynical. "I don't make friends lightly. I *knew* Bill. If there was anything left of him, he would let me know."

"If you're suggesting we're talking about a split personality, that there was a struggle for control, and that Mark Kingdom came out on top, what I need to establish is: How much of an intruder was Mark Kingdom; had he always been in Ingham's subconscious, or was he some 'alien' personality who simply muscled in?"

Kester laughed. "Alien personality? You've been reading too much science fiction. He was a figment of our imagination!"

"I don't understand. . . ."

He seemed surprised. "I thought you knew. I'd better tell you how it happened. . . ."

I don't know whether you have any idea of what it's like to run a column like mine [Kester said]. At times it's a nightmare. I'm bombarded with material, but believe it or not, I've got pretty high standards, and sometimes I almost despair of filling the page. On that day Bill called in, as he said, to *hide* from Joe Lestrange, the news editor, because he didn't fancy being sent out on a story when he was due to finish in ten minutes. I recall ribbing him because there had been a time when the job came first, but since his marriage there were signs of him becoming henpecked. Magda meant well but she tended to mother him . . . seems strange, referring to a gorgeous creature like her in those terms, but she was a little possessive.

He could see I was stuck for inspiration, and was trying to help in a half-serious, half-kidding fashion—sorting through a pile of papers, press releases, and pictures on my desk. News reporters don't have to think all that deeply; the facts are there, or have to be uncovered, and they merely report or interpret; so he found it hard to accept that from that huge wad of material, I couldn't find a line for the column. In fact, most of it was either free publicity for some product that could well afford to pay for advertising space, or a puff for some small-time actor or actress who off their own bat couldn't say or do anything that was worth printing. . . . I regarded the whole lot as so much toilet paper, but Bill was very taken with some young dolly bird . . . you can imagine the type of photo, leaving very little to the imagination. Our tastes, if he was serious, were so far apart, I appealed to him to let me choose my own material.

He reminded me that it was I who had been moaning. "If you've got such Olympian standards, you'll never find anything acceptable," he said. "You'll have to make it up. When I worked on the agency, we were always making up 'news' stories to put out when there was nothing happening. I remember doing a fog story one year. We had people queuing up to vote in a by-election. . . ."

I yawned theatrically to put him off, but he insisted on making the point: "Oh, there *was* a by-election—my little twist in the tail was that when voters groped their way to the front of the line, they found they'd been queuing for fish and chips. We didn't find out until later that there were no fish-and-chip shops in that area, but it was only meant as a 'filler,' and most papers used it."

"And the moral is. . . ?"

He shrugged. "There isn't one. I'm just saying it was an amusing little piece and quite harmless."

Partly to appease him, I offered to buy a topical fog story, but he backed down and said he would have to wait for inspiration. But he was thinking like mad, and within a matter of seconds he had an idea. He asked if I read our book reviews. "We carried one a couple of months ago," he pointed out. "A documentary collection of stories about the so-called messiahs, hot gospelers and faith healers. Fabulous *characters* like Father Divine. They always make good copy, and it's a fascinating subject; why don't you do a piece about a new messiah?"

The topic amused me. *"Who,* for example? Do you know any suitable candidates?"

He was serious now. "Make him up! You know how gullible some people are. . . . What's the betting you'd even get some cranks wanting to join your imaginary Band of Hope?"

My heart sank. The idea had intrigued me, but Bill's suggestion was rather more dishonest than I'd bargained for. I like to feel I've got a sort of responsibility to my public. A small one, admittedly, but a responsibility nevertheless. I explained the difference between a fictitious news paragraph tucked away, and my page. "Apart from the fact that your fog story was harmless and past tense, the vast news machine is an anonymous entity. People who read my page identify the contents with me. Perhaps I'm being romantic, but in a sense they trust me, and this item may not be as harmless as it sounds."

"Why ever not?" he protested. "Look, for the sake of simplicity, let's say that one of those press handouts is from the new messiah—or rather, the guy claiming to be . . . could be *anyone.* Could be me. I tell you my story and you carry it for what it's worth. As an impartial observer, you neither praise nor decry me. . . ."

"You don't have to tell me what to say—just convince me that it's harmless," I said.

He was exasperated at my extreme caution. "Surely . . . I mean, what reaction *could* there be? Either none at all or, as I suggested, you'll get a few letters from cranks—which you could conveniently lose. . . ."

Since we often get completely incoherent and cranky letters that are filed in the wastepaper basket, the suggestion was not so unreasonable, and I found myself weakening. Bill was indifferent to that sort of detail and his brain was racing ahead, trying to think of a name. He thought aloud, several outlandish names cropping up until he was happy with "Father Supreme."

I thought that sounded more like a custard powder and began to work on the problem myself. "You need to have some connection with God, or Jesus, or the Kingdom of Heaven," I suggested. "Problem is, the best ones have probably all been taken. . . ."

"What's wrong with *Kingdom* for a surname?" he said.

"Could be . . . although it's a bit pop-singerish—Johnny Kingdom and his seven sinners!"

He disagreed. "It would sound all right if the Christian name was appropriate. Something like . . . Matthew . . . Luke . . ."

I thought that was hilarious. Luke Kingdom? Sounded like a hillbilly. We tried our initials, and then those of our wives: Magda and Rosalind. M. I. and R. K. spelled *MIRK* . . . which sounded appropriate.

Bill was ahead of me. "Or 'S. Mirk, the Savior with the Sunny Smile.' But I was thinking of something a trifle more sober. Let's just alter the *i* to *a,* and make it *MARK.* Mark Kingdom."

That suited me, so we moved on to the question of a platform, preferably a new tack, but Bill pointed out that if we decided on something too offbeat, the other papers would smell a story and follow it up. It was safer to make him rather less sensational, so we favored an air of mystery, which would kill two birds with one stone.

Anyway, I carried a fairly innocuous piece in the column, although the response was not quite what we had anticipated. I took a couple of the letters when Ros and I went to the Inghams' for dinner, because Bill hadn't been in the office and might not be even the next day. We'd been joking about the piece, which the girls hadn't particularly noticed, and I was irritated with Ros because she wouldn't have been impressed if I carried an interview with Saint Peter. She must have been having a go at me that night, because when I produced the letter she made some crack about it being unethical.

Magda was on my side. "If people are unbalanced enough to write to crazy hot gospelers they've never seen—and probably never *heard* of—they don't deserve to be treated seriously," she said.

I admitted that letters were normally treated as confidential but that I was making an exception in this case because it had been Bill's idea to write up Mark Kingdom and he was therefore entitled to know the response. ". . . Especially as it's not altogether what you expected," I said. "Most of them ran true to pattern, but three or four were rather surprising."

He read the letter in silence while the girls ribbed him impatiently. And when he had finished he was shaken, admitting that it had taken the wind out of his sails. He was even reluctant to let the girls see it. "It's written by someone pretty close to despair," he explained, "and I don't think we've got any right to mock her. It's really rather pathetic."

Magda was unmoved. "*All* cranks are pathetic," she said, "or funny, depending which way you look at it. . . ."

"Or just plain warped," Ros chipped in. "What about the crazy bunch who thought Hitler was the messiah?"

Bill was reluctant to read it aloud, insisting that it was a *private* communication, but I reminded him that it was he who had prompted the writer to send it. I can't remember the text in detail, but basically it was a description of how this girl had been paralyzed from the waist down by polio. In a resigned and unemotional manner she described the way she had recently been getting fresh pains in her arms and shoulders and suspected that the paralysis was spreading. The doctors had been noncommittal, and she was now desperate. There was one particularly haunting phrase about not asking for miracles—only hope.

I was intensely embarrassed and the girls were moved. They examined the handwriting and Ros decided that this seemed a perfectly normal girl at her wits' end, although Magda was not convinced—she suggested that it would not be the first time a permanent physical incapacity had unbalanced a healthy mind.

We got into a discussion over the differences between genuine and psychosomatic symptoms, and the difference between psychiatrists and faith healers. Stupidly, as it transpired, I put in a word for the faith healers—merely intending to stimulate the argument. I said we automatically called them charlatans, yet seldom investigated their claims as individuals. "I'm convinced that a few faith healers get results," I said. "After all, how was Christ able to accomplish what he did? Unless you believe he was the son of God . . . in which case he comes under the category of Messiah. . . ."

Ros qualified my remark. "I think the danger generally is that too many people—gullible people—put their faith in intangibles." She looked at Ingham for a reaction, but he seemed to be too depressed to respond.

Magda was sympathetic but pressed him with a question about how he would react if they had a daughter who was suffering from something terrible; would he take her to a hospital—or to a faith healer?

"Well, obviously . . . ," he hedged, "we know what *we'd* do, but this girl has already seen all the specialists, and now she has no one . . ."

"Except Mark Kingdom?" asked Magda. "What makes you think he can help?"

It wasn't possible to remain silent, and with as much emphasis as I could, I pointed out that he certainly could not.

Bill kept his head down, blatantly ignoring my comment. "In the general sense I've no more belief in these characters than you have," he maintained. "But it seems logical that if all else has failed, she loses nothing by transferring her faith elsewhere—*anywhere,* even to a lucky charm, if you believe faith has any value. . . ."

"It doesn't necessarily *follow* that she loses nothing," Ros said. "While there's life, there's hope—and they might even find some new wonder drug. We don't really know enough about this poor girl, but it's fair to say that one shouldn't tamper with the unknown. Faith is a form of hypnosis. You can tell a person that he's not in pain, and he might believe it, but that doesn't stop cancer killing him. . . ."

"At least he's not in pain—that's something, surely?" Bill argued.

I tried to disillusion him. "He still *dies!* You might just as well have put him to sleep—euthanasia also has its advocates."

I assumed Magda dismissed the idea once and for all when she pointed out that the girl did not seem to have any money of her own, and that if Kingdom ran true to type, it was unlikely she'd melt his heart. But Bill had a bee in his bonnet, and next day he started driving me mad about the girl's letter.

I tried to shake him off, pointing out that if he wanted to make exceptions, we had two others in a similar vein, possibly a third. "You seem to forget that Kingdom doesn't even exist—except in our imagination," I reminded him.

"But *they* think he does," he argued.

"So what are you suggesting now? That *I* write to them on his behalf? You must be mad—I'm sorry I ever agreed to the stupid bloody idea!"

"No more than I am; I couldn't have had more than half an hour's sleep all night. We started this mess, George. We thought we were being clever. . . ."

"So. . . ?"

"If you start a fire, you ought to put it out!"

"It'll have to burn *itself* out," I said. "If we do anything else now, we'll only fan the flames."

He wouldn't listen, and eventually, in exasperation, I suggested that—if being in it up to his neck was not deep enough—he could go the whole hog and answer the letters himself. Even then I didn't think he really would. I tried other tacks, including ridicule, but nothing seemed to work. "Tell me what *harm* it can do," he argued. "I give you my word I'll back off at the first opportunity."

"You mean you'll tell them in advance that miracles take a little longer," I said. "They'll understand the problem. . . ."

With considerable bad grace I capitulated and gave him the four most coherent letters, intending to get rid of the rest. I asked him what he had to offer these people and he couldn't really answer, muttering vaguely about hope . . . confidence in themselves . . . platitudes. . . . It made me furious. "Hope? You're already their last hope," I said. "They haven't really despaired yet—and they won't, until they realize that you can't deliver. What's going to happen then?"

The telephone, summoning him to the news desk, prevented the situation from blowing up into a full-scale row, but that was the start of the rift between us.

After that he seemed to keep out of my way, and the next thing I knew was Mackay going berserk just before the Seeley story broke. Apparently, as a matter of courtesy, the Press Association sent a personal memo to him about the apparent double life of one of his reporters, before releasing their story on the "miracle" cure. Being an alert man, he immediately identified the name Kingdom with the piece I'd carried, so it wasn't long before he had the full story. You know Mackay—the paper always comes first, so his main consideration was not so much what we'd done, but how he was going to explain it.

You've never seen Mackay in a rage, but take it from me, it's an awesome sight. Yet the remarkable thing was that, with me literally trembling in my boots, Bill was quite unmoved and radiating the serenity (smugness in my book) of a holy man. He tried to get me off the hook by conceding that I had not been involved since writing the original piece, but that made the old man even angrier.

"Don't waste my time with that boy scout drivel!" he yelled. "What Kester did was bad enough, but once he realized the joke had misfired, he should have come to me instead of keeping quiet."

Bill told him quite complacently that he doubted whether he would have listened to him any more than he had me, and I squirmed in anticipation of Mackay's reaction. He was like a simmering volcano. "Doubt, do you? Well, *your* doubting days are over. If you value your job at all, you'll do as you're told in future."

That seemed to get through to Bill because he announced he would continue to take orders as long as they didn't affect his personal life. He maintained that as Mark Kingdom he had acted on his own initiative and in his own time—that he was not a slave to the paper twenty-four hours a day. . . .

Mackay argued that this did not help him with what the *Chronicle* was supposed to print.

"Why not just print the truth?" Bill asked. "Apart from the beginning, which was a trick, admittedly—and you can always say that George didn't know that Mark Kingdom wasn't a real person—the rest can be the facts. . . ."

"That still leaves one of my reporters a con-merchant," Mackay said.

"I deny that. The only deception has been in the name. Otherwise I've done nothing that would embarrass the paper. I've never taken a penny from anyone. . . ."

Mackay seemed to be impressed with that argument, but I was not. "You're still posing as someone with supernatural powers!" I insisted.

"I've never claimed anything of the sort. . . ."

"Perhaps not, but the inference is there."

"And now the proof, perhaps. . . ?" he replied.

I found it impossible to control my temper. "I thought as much! You're beginning to believe it yourself!" I threw in a few personal insults for good measure, but he stayed calm, and eventually Mackay told *me* to sit down. As I said, to him the truth was less important than the paper's good name, so he was prepared to accept Bill's suggestion.

"A little controversy never did anyone any harm," he said. "We'll carry an editorial stating that the paper must reserve judgment until further evidence is available. . . . Kingdom could well be what he claims, or a fake . . . readers meanwhile must judge for themselves."

It was all very well trying to get the paper off the hook, but I knew that my innocuous little paragraph about Mark

Kingdom had inspired eight or nine people to write in. With a splash like the one he was forecasting, and talk of miracles, we'd be getting eight or nine hundred! Yet Mackay already had his mind on other aspects, and when I warned him of the danger he shrugged it off, as though it were Ingham's problem, maintaining he would deal with it if and when it arose.

I cherished no illusions about our bosses, but I felt sick. "You're a thousand times more dishonest than I am."

He laughed. "Perhaps that's why I am an editor, and you're only a columnist. . . !"

"Everyone's so busy hurling accusations around that no one's even entertained the idea that Mark Kingdom might just have certain powers," Bill interjected.

I told him that I'd never believed in miracles, and I saw no reason to start now. He asked how I accounted for Jessica, and before I could answer, he submitted his own case.

"The specialists said there was *no* chance of her ever re-gaining any movement in her legs," he said. "I saw those legs, and didn't have to be a medical man to *know* they were dead. But the other night they came to life; she *used* them. The *doctor* called it a miracle. . . . It'll be months, possibly six months before she can walk properly, but there's life there. . . ."

Mackay switched his attention back to us. "What I'd like to know, as a father, is if you've never had any reason to believe in these powers before, why should you suddenly develop them?"

Bill admitted he had no idea, but suggested that perhaps it was because the challenge had never arisen until . . .

I butted in: ". . . until one day you thought what a good joke it would make. . . ."

"Yes, that might be true," he admitted, "but equally it could also have been God's way of forcing my hand. Ever since the night you came to dinner, I've felt I was being propelled along this path by some force outside my control."

Mackay asked if that meant he intended to carry on, and Bill agreed, ". . . as long as people need me . . ."

". . . or until you do irreparable harm?" I replied. "All right, so the *Chronicle* stays on the fence, but what about the other nationals? What is there to stop someone doing an exposé—it's perfectly normal practice, and they'd have every justification. . . ."

He said they would get nothing on him, which I found laughable. "You're joking, of course! What about your pals on the *Daily Record;* if one of these boys starts to dig . . ." I broke off because there seemed little point in rubbing it in—messiahs and faith healers were easy meat; he had said so himself. . . .

He tried to tell us that he was different, he was sincere. God!

Anyway, you've probably seen the cuttings. Success, if you call it that, brought more success. He got himself organized, hired himself that PR man and all the trappings, and launched Mark Kingdom formally at a press conference at his flat—which I just had to attend. Give him credit, he handled himself pretty well; just the right balance of friendliness and authority, to remind us that he was a very different Bill Ingham from the man some of us had regarded as a boozing companion. Sensibly he'd prepared for the obviously "loaded" questions. For example, he was able to give chapter and verse about *gifted* men, as he modestly called them, who had not revealed their powers until late in

life . . . Muhammad, at the age of forty . . . Saint Ignatius
Loyola, founder of the Jesuits, in his thirties. . . .

He had quite a telling point about the acceptance of fate
being a very personal thing, and that because of the very
size and ambiguity of the Church, there are few points of
personal contact for the individual. In the Catholic Church,
the priest often provides such a link, but is limited by the
restriction of dogma.

I'd deliberately arrived late so that we wouldn't have an
opportunity to speak first, and we merely acknowledged
each other from opposite sides of the room. As I'd hoped,
he was evidently more intrigued with my companion, because she was to be my "ace in the hole." I allowed the
others to do the questioning for most of the conference because I had another trick up my sleeve, and because they
had prepared their answers too well, but his composure irritated me.

Eventually I had to make a comment about the financial
rewards available to the successful healer, saying that I
trusted he would not allow riches to spoil him, but my sarcasm was wasted. He and Leighton had their answers off
pat. In fact, his PR man was such a smooth operator, he
was able to close the meeting on a high point: He invited
us to continue our discussions over drinks, knowing that
only a couple of the more serious journalists would bother
to pursue their questioning, and confident that Bill could
handle them in isolation.

My companion, ostensibly my secretary/assistant—although I wouldn't have expected anyone to believe that in a
thousand years—was an incredibly sexy-looking starlet
called Sonya Douglas, whose immediate ambition was to
get her photograph on my page. She and her agent had been
trying for years, and now I'd capitulated in exchange for a

small favor, which was why she was here. The other guys clustered round her like bees round a honey pot, but she'd been well briefed . . . friendly, but keeping her distance. We hung around, drinking until there was only Phil Kane of the *Record* left, and I was determined to outstay him. The PR man dropped a few hints about the time, but Kane was reluctant to leave me a clear pitch until I managed to persuade him that my reasons for hanging on were purely social. The PR man evidently decided I was reasonably harmless, and having failed to pry Sonya away, took the hint and left with Kane.

Bill had put back a few drinks, and although he was far from being drunk, his guard had dropped fractionally. As long as we were not alone, I would not provoke a serious row, and there was no doubt he was taken with Sonya. I had been looking for a chink in his armor, and I hoped this was it. There was something familiar about her face and jutting bust line, but out of her environment he was unable to place her, and she'd been instructed to conceal the fact that she was an actress. . . .

I'd hit on using Sonya because it was her photograph he'd been fascinated by the day we had come up with the Mark Kingdom idea. I get a dozen or so similar pics a week, but he had practically drooled over it, trying to convince me that I was missing my opportunities and that girls like Sonya were only too glad to demonstrate their "gratitude" for a puff in my column. He had changed considerably in recent months, but I was pretty sure he would respond to her in the right circumstances. With Magda gone, he was undoubtedly lonely . . . and the flat was private enough . . . and Sonya was consolation for any man. The room was hot and stuffy and I told her to take her jacket off; and if I say so myself, she did look pretty irresistible. Telling Bill that she had twisted my arm to bring her because she wanted to meet him, I poured us all another "last" drink and watched her get to work on him. Frankly, it must have been a bit corny, but he didn't seem to notice, reminding us, in fact, of the sacrificial lamb. In due course I looked at my watch somewhat obviously and announced that I had to leave for an appointment. By that time he was as randy as a stallion and hardly noticed, so I left him to it . . . to spread his gospel, no doubt!

I had been stunned by Kester's revelations. Ingham had begun his story with Jessica's cure. It was unlikely he had forgotten the dishonest way it had all begun, yet it may well have been censored by his subconscious. Nevertheless, he had some explaining to do.

Meanwhile, Kester's condemnation—one might even describe it as "gloating"—of the events after the press conference seemed out of character for a man who struck me as being a cool customer. Something rankled, something he had not mentioned. After all, I asked him, what was so awful about a reasonably unsophisticated yet apparently virile man being laid by an attractive semi-pro? Kester had shrugged, I thought slightly embarrassed. "Nothing—if he hadn't been posing as a saint," he replied.

But even a saint might be caught off-guard when the trap was baited with such determination. Why did he seem so triumphant at having put one over on his former friend?

61

"Nothing you've said has basically changed my impression of him," I asserted. "The only allegation that might be made to stick is perhaps complacency—something his friends might call 'serenity.'"

He was quiet for a few seconds and then grinned sheepishly. "Perhaps it's just that . . . I can't abide serenity!"

There had to be another reason, possibly jealousy of one sort or another, although whether this was significant was another matter.

My next appointment was with Norah Peters, a pleasant prospect in more ways than one. As a bookseller, particularly when I'm working on catalogs, which I believe should be more than just a listing of titles with brief description, I have a constant need for access to rare antiquarian books and manuscripts. I do much of this research at the National Bibliographical Library; while its coverage is nowhere near as comprehensive as that of the better-known British Library, I prefer its more intimate atmosphere.

Naturally, I had no reason during these visits to call in on the bindery, which was Ms. Peters' preserve, but we had met socially, although I doubted whether she would remember me. The occasion had been one of the monthly receptions given by Wilfred Frensham, one of London's most distinguished antiquarian booksellers, and a former president of the Antiquarian Booksellers' Association. I was fortunate, on joining the trade, in having gained Frensham's friendship, and my name was usually on his guest list.

Norah Peters is not the sort of person one easily forgets. A history graduate with a love of art and craftsmanship, she was not only an authority on fine bookbinding, but stunningly attractive; an almost flawless honey-blonde. Yet despite her looks I had found her surprisingly sexless; an instinctive impression I can't explain—after all, she was friendly enough—but it may have had something to do with her seriousness, not to say single-mindedness. I could not imagine her having any interest outside old books, their repair and conservation. But how wrong my hunch had been! Just the same, it had been apparent that other men had been attracted. Wilfred, for example, who was something of a connoisseur and who had already been smitten by Laura, was a great admirer.

I used Wilfred's cocktail party several months earlier as an icebreaker, and if she only pretended to remember our meeting it was friendly enough until I brought up the sub-ject of Mark Kingdom, when she visibly froze, a slow red flush suffusing her delicate fair complexion.

Hastening to reassure her, I explained my special interest, after which she relaxed perceptibly. She told me what I al-ready knew—that she had not seen Ingham since his disap-pearance.

"I'm more interested in the period before Jessica Seeley's death," I pointed out. "I've spoken to Doug Leighton, his campaign manager, and to George Kester, the columnist on the *Daily Chronicle*—both of whom I'd expect to know him intimately—and they might have been talking about two different people. If he is a split personality, which of them is the person you know and, presumably, love?"

"Who told you about me?" she inquired, straining to ap-pear casual.

"Leighton. Was it supposed to be a secret?"

She ignored the question. "The man I know is real enough for me. I don't care what other names he has."

"Do you think he murdered the girl?"

"Why do I feel like crying, when it is all so ludicrous?"

"You tell me."

She shrugged. "Whatever happens now, they've de-

stroyed his life. All he ever tried to do was to help people—
and how was he repaid? His wife walked out on him . . .
and the little angel, Jessica, turned out to be a devil. One
way or another, all of his friends exploited him. . . ."

"What does that mean? Explain."

"I can't. Only he could tell you. I can only guess, but it's
too painful. He's the only man I've ever loved—the only
man I would dream of marrying—and now he is probably
lying at the bottom of some river."

I played a hunch. "How would you react if I told you he
was alive, and I knew how to contact him?"

Her eyes widened, and the flush reappeared to creep up
her neck.

"I can't promise anything, but if I can produce him, I'd
like you to be there so that you can fill in some of the gaps
there may be in his memory. Would you do that?"

She nodded.

During the short conversation with Norah Peters I had
come to the conclusion that Ingham had left too many questions unanswered. To some extent it had been my fault in
insisting on just the bare essentials; we had both been tired.
But now I needed him to put the stories of Leighton and
Kester in perspective before taking the investigation any further. And since I had discovered nothing that cleared him of
suspicion, he could not be sheltered from the police for
much longer.

The logical course was to get Ingham back to London,
where I could see him at Laura's flat, ideally when she was
on hand to monitor my reactions. I was not pleased with
my progress, and fancied she might spot something I had
missed. Ingham was not too happy at the prospect of returning to where he might have to face the music, but he

was still too passive to argue; in any case, he seemed to have a childlike faith in my ability to resolve his problems. Laura offered no objection, unconcerned by my warning that she was at risk of joining me in becoming an accessory—if he should subsequently be charged.

When Ingham arrived, he still seemed in something of a daze. Apparently oblivious of his surroundings, he acknowledged Laura vaguely, almost rudely, as though taking her involvement for granted. Even more striking was his passive acquiescence to Norah's emotional welcome. He seemed to regard her embrace as an obligation to be suffered, yet Norah did not seem to be aware of his coldness— or, if she did, she did not show it.

I sat Ingham down in an armchair with a double Scotch that he accepted with a bemused smile, and pulled up a high-backed chair so that I was facing him only a couple of feet away. Laura and Norah sat at right angles to us, and I signaled with a glance that I hoped to establish a rapport that might be broken if we interrupted. Then I produced the list of questions I'd prepared and started at the top. "When did you first meet Jessica Seeley?"

There was a normal reaction at last because an expression of mild surprise almost animated his face. "Isn't the *last* time rather more relevant?" he inquired. "That's what they usually ask."

"I know that already."

"But that is all the police care about . . . when I'm supposed to have killed her. And since there was no one else in the room at the time, the hypothesis is not all that unreasonable."

"But you have no recollection of actually killing her?" I persisted, irritable at his apparent indifference. "You had no *motive* for killing her?"

He raised an eyebrow. "What has motive got to do with it? They'll say I was juiced up to the eyebrows, or round the twist—whichever sounds worst. The best I can hope for is mitigation—what they call 'diminished responsibility'—and get twenty years in Broadmoor. . . ."

I ignored the prediction but queried his speculation about the prosecution line. "Were you. . . ?"

"Was I what?"

"Juiced up—or round the twist. . . ?"

I could sense that Ingham was beginning to respond to my questions. The trauma of recent events had acted as a powerful anesthetic, but his mental state was an issue vital to the defense; indeed, his life might depend on it. When he eventually replied, it was apparent the question had been evaluated very carefully.

"I'm certain of one thing—I've never consciously taken drugs," he said. "I don't know about the rest—there must be a fairly strong possibility I'm mentally unbalanced. . . ."

"If you're talking about split personality, that's something the medical experts can argue the toss about. Meanwhile, there is a jigsaw to be put together and quite a few missing pieces—so let's see if we can start establishing some positive link between your behavior pattern over the past few months and the girl's death. I'd like to know how it all began."

"You really mean the first meeting?"

I nodded, and he thought for a moment before prefacing his remarks with an ironic snort.

"It might never have happened!" he said. "Her parents didn't want to let me in, but she heard us arguing at the front door and called out. She was used to getting her own way—an only child, born when they were already middle-aged. Some sort of guilt complex perhaps. Probably didn't

want a child, and when she was crippled, assumed it was
God's will to punish them, so they overcompensated. If
they had stood up to her that night, put a foot down firmly
and refused to let me in, she might have been alive today."

"How can you say that? You made her walk . . . something the doctors said was impossible."

"Oh, the miracle. . . ?" He laughed. "Sure, I performed
miracles. So did Jesus, and look where it got him."

It was impossible to fathom at that stage whether he was
serious, or mad, or mocking me (perhaps even himself), so
I modulated my tone very carefully in phrasing the next
question. "She walked. *You* were responsible, according to
the girl, her parents—even the doctors. No one can take
that away."

"Perhaps *I* did," he replied without any hint of self-pity.

"We're jumping ahead. Tell me about that first meeting—
after they let you in. . . ." I sat back, took out my notebook, and asked him to start. Nobody until now really
knew the whole story.

I remember it vividly [began Ingham]; hardly surprising,
since it was the day that changed my life. I'd called at the
Seeleys' flat (one of those rather swish blocks round the corner to St. John's Wood station) after work, and the old man
answered the door . . . nice guy, although his wife is a pain
in the arse. *She* even wanted to call the police . . . seems a
friend had read the piece about Mark Kingdom and she was
scared of the child's head being filled with a lot of "mumbo
jumbo," as she put it, about faith healers. She always referred to Jessica as "the child," although, as you probably
know, she was in her early twenties.

Anyway, it was touch and go until Jessica called out and I
tipped the scales by volunteering to let them stay with

us. . . . Jessica was sitting in a wheelchair, but the first thing I noticed was her exceptional face. If anything, she was too pretty, almost doll-like. The rest of her body was completely sexless, and her legs were a bit off-putting, in fact. However, I'd been touched by her letter and was too full of compassion to feel any sort of repugnance. I know that probably sounds hypocritical, since I was perpetuating an illusion, pretending to be a faith healer who did not exist, but all I wanted was to give her a few crumbs of comfort, before leaving as gracefully as possible. I should have realized at that moment that she was not the sort of person to let go, but that's being wise after the event.

There were actually tears of happiness in her eyes when she thanked me for coming, and although I was moved by her gratitude, I found I had to keep a straight face a moment later when she said she had pictured me the way I was.

I was very conscious of my inadequacy, and how much I had underestimated the degree of involvement that would be required of me. Yet, when simply to break the ice, I asked how she was feeling, you would have thought I'd said something terribly profound.

The expression was radiant. "Wonderful," she cried. "The pains in my arms began to disappear the moment I got your letter. . . ."

You've probably heard that she had been paralyzed from the waist down after an attack of polio at the age of sixteen, but what isn't generally known is that Jessica had written to Mark Kingdom because she was terrified the paralysis might be spreading to her arms. The doctors could find nothing wrong, nor could they offer an explanation for the mystery pains. It seemed too good to be true, and I asked if there had been any recurrence.

Apparently there had, but she was prepared to dismiss it.

"The day after I'd written my second letter to you, it suddenly occurred to me how much I was taking for granted—and that perhaps you wouldn't come. The pains came back almost immediately. But when I forced myself to brush aside the doubts, they went off again. I haven't felt so brimming with hope for years."

I remarked that it seemed evident the pains must have been in some way related to her mood and thoughts, so that in theory there was no reason why they should ever return, and her answer surprised me.

"I've been aware of that for some time," she admitted. "The last specialist Daddy took me to said he could find nothing wrong with my arms and that the trouble lay in my mind. He talked to me like a Dutch uncle, said that only *I* could overcome them. But I knew from the start that willpower alone wasn't enough. I needed help from *outside*."

"Why are you so certain I can help?" I asked.

She was utterly convinced. "You have already. If I never saw you again, I would still have gained something. But if I can go *on* seeing you, I'll get completely better . . . I know it."

What could I say? There I was trying to get off the hook at the first opportunity, while she was dreaming of regular contact. I recall making some trite comment about leaving it in God's hands.

She said that she believed faith could move mountains. "If you were to tell me that it was God's will I should die tomorrow, I should die tomorrow contentedly. All I shall ever ask of you is inspiration, or merely guidance."

I was relieved that there were apparent limits to her expectations of me, so I was able to speak with a little more confidence. "You mustn't think of me as anything special,"

I said, "but as a friend. And as a friend I shall give what little I can willingly—guidance . . . my strength . . . and my will. . . ."

I managed to avoid embarrassing areas, such as prayer— persuading her, for example, that it should be a personal and *mental* communication, and she seemed to accept that, although it was obvious she was concerned more at this moment with seeing me. "You will call again?" she begged. I hesitated. Perhaps it might be easier to get out of it later, and I agreed to call a few days later. Then I gave her a bit of a pep talk and said she must start learning to have faith in herself.

She promised to try. But of course, I was hooked. I thought, "just one evening," and then it was just one more. The problem was she really depended on me. She listened to everything I said as though it were the Gospel, and although initially I restricted my advice to basic common sense, and what I think was a reasonably down-to-earth philosophy, if I had said it was in her power to fly, she would have jumped out of the window happily.

I found myself sneaking out at night to see her and a fine old man, Ben Lawton, telling my wife I was working late at the office. I might not have had the incentive if they were not so obviously benefiting from the visits. It had a snow-balling effect, so that everything I did seemed to have been preordained. For example, compared with Jessica, the old man was pretty undemanding, and I felt I wanted to do something extra for him. As a start, there seemed no harm in massaging his arms—and to my surprise the pain and stiffness just seemed to evaporate. So what worked with him was naturally tried on Jessica, in her father's presence, and (over a longer period because her legs had been dead for nearly seven years) the effect was even more startling.

The crunch came with a phone call late one night from Mr. Seeley . . . Jessica was able to stand. I forced them to take medical advice, and within twenty-four hours we knew something wonderful had happened. There was no scientific explanation.

Of course, when the story broke, I was in trouble. It was a "natural" . . . pretty young cripple girl given up by the doctors and saved by a mystery healer . . . and, to make matters more complicated, the name Mark Kingdom was a phony. The editor blew up . . . not a word about the cure . . . only concerned that the paper was going to be shown in a bad light. Magda was, I think, genuinely pleased for the girl—but realized I was beginning to be dragged away by circumstances beyond our control.

To give you an example: A few nights later, a young couple knocked at the door with a sick baby. The baby was obviously very ill; they were completely distraught and refused to listen to our automatic advice—to take the child to a hospital. They had heard about Jessica and the so-called "miracle," and begged me to cure the baby by laying on my hands. What could I do? Throw them out? Magda was sickened, and I must admit I was horribly embarrassed, but I did the only thing I could . . . placed my hands on the baby's head and prayed aloud. Only then could I persuade them to go straight to the hospital. We checked next morning, and there was an improvement in the baby's condition. Nobody could persuade those parents it was an oxygen tent and antibiotics and not divine help that saved him, and that was typical of the sort of situation I was beginning to find myself in.

It was probably that incident which made Magda decide to leave me. Ironically, what she or any of my friends seemed unable to accept was the possibility that I *did* have some gift of healing. The fact that for the first thirty years of my life there had been no evidence is beside the point. . . .

My work for the paper had been suffering, and the morning after Magda left I overslept, was late for an assignment, and generally made a balls-up of something important. So I was suddenly out. I found myself minus a wife and job, and it seemed logical to give in to Mr. Seeley's entreaties and allow him and a few friends to put up some money. They looked around for a campaign manager, and Doug Leighton conveniently appeared on the scene with the necessary qualifications. As he was also a friend of my ex–news editor, we didn't look any further.

I don't really know how much I was carried along by the tide of events and how much I anticipated them and prepared myself accordingly. I had never even opened the Bible until I met Jessica, when I began to dip into it for suitable references. Gradually I found it useful to trot out a quotation or two—stopped me from having to think all the time of something profound to say. So in a way, I suppose, I was becoming the sort of phony I despised, although my motives were always sincere. In fact, I was changing so much, I couldn't help wondering just how far from the "real" me the new public image would eventually be.

I couldn't help liking Doug, although once I'd given an inch, he expected a yard. The more involved he became and the more he was able to contribute, the more relaxed, natural, and even outrageous he became. On one occasion Seeley was sorting through checks and postal orders from well-wishers, and I had another strong pang of conscience over accepting money from poor fools who didn't know me from Adam. Doug said I should read the letters before judging and asked if he could have them because every writer should receive invitations to our meetings.

I recall making some crack about "cranks," and he said, "No such thing—only good money and bad money from now on. . . !"

Seeley was shocked, but Doug's laugh was so infectious, we couldn't take him seriously.

Meanwhile, I was beginning to have problems with Jessica, possessive and jealous of the time I was spending on plans for the launch. In my absence she would work herself up into varying degrees of hysteria and then begin to experience pain in her arms and legs—so that I'd get a panic-stricken call from her stupid mother. I knew it was psychosomatic, but she was spoiled and unreasonable. Yet, strangely enough, although she had this obsession about me being with her . . . about this spiritual bond between us . . . she was alone in recognizing the change in me—that I was in effect conforming in advance to the image Doug was cultivating. She was too self-centered to care about the reason, but she certainly hit the nail on the head. . . .

I'd been protesting that I couldn't be at her beck and call. She didn't need me there all the time; if necessary, she could use the telephone. But when she got emotional, I was suddenly drained of coherent thought. I'd simply run out of sensible arguments, so I fell back on a handy quote from the Bible: "If thou faint in the day of adversity, thy strength is small," which comes from Proverbs. I pointed out that she had already demonstrated her strength and that it would be tragic to falter now.

She calmed down and regarded me soberly. "I suppose it's because I'm so tired of fighting . . . tired of being an object of pity and curiosity. Why can't I be normal like other people?"

I kidded her out of feeling sorry for herself, but then she asked whether Magda might come back. She didn't know about Norah.

"Probably not," I said. "It isn't easy for a woman."

That made her angry. "Not for her type. She's a *model,* isn't she?"

The transparent jealousy was amusing, and I laughed. "One of the best . . ."

She was hurt. "You don't seem very concerned. She betrayed you, but you still defend her."

There was little point in arguing with her in that mood, but she must have interpreted my silence as another indication of my nobility of character, because she climbed out of the chair and came toward me. She wasn't yet really steady on her legs and I was scared she might fall, but she was single-minded enough to make it, although she allowed me to help her back. Jessica was due to go into the hospital in a fortnight for intensive physiotherapy, which I knew would work wonders, and I reminded her of the benefits. Determination registered on her face. "By the time I come out . . . it may take months, admittedly . . . I'll be a normal woman."

I agreed, and looked at my watch, conscious of the fact that I couldn't spare any more time merely boosting her morale. An awareness of my thoughts must have alarmed her because she suddenly announced that her legs were aching. It was mentioned innocently enough—in fact, it was accompanied by an embarrassed laugh. "It's nothing much," she said, "I expect I've been overdoing it."

That was probably true. It was only natural that she should be impatient to catch up. Instinctively I knelt and massaged the flesh around her knees. Jessica relaxed immediately, lulling me into a sense of false security, so that when she took my hand I hardly noticed. But when she moved it between her legs—right to the top—I jumped as though I'd been scalded.

I remember losing my temper and calling her a bitch, but she was unabashed. I'd honestly only ever thought of her as a patient, but now, when I'd made it doubly clear, she dismissed it as a "Victorian" attitude—something that applied to the "common" people, perhaps, but hardly to men of my stature. I didn't know whether to laugh or cry, and made matters worse by threatening to tell her parents unless she promised never to try again. Her face contorted with frustration and rage. "It was *you* . . . you were always making advances," she said, and looked at me calculatingly. "See which of us they'll believe. . . ."

I didn't have a leg to stand on, and when I started to leave, she called me back with a soft but bitter parting thrust. "I might tell them anyway, so you'd better not neglect me anymore. I'll see you tomorrow. . . ."

I reminded her that I would be busy with my speech and couldn't spare the time, but it was an ultimatum, and I realized she had the whip hand. There was no one I could tell— not even Norah.

The first meeting was a pretty traumatic experience, as you may have heard. I was beginning to show the strain from this incredibly bizarre existence—initially the struggle between Bill Ingham and Mark Kingdom, the unpleasant experience with Jessica, and finally the nightmare of the meeting. I hadn't been sleeping well, and now I started getting hallucinations—which good old Doug attributed to divine inspiration. At first I didn't know whether to doubt *his* sanity or mine, but I soon came to terms even with that supposition. The hallucinations, after all, were completely out of this world, and if one accepted that I might have some gift of healing, then who could say that the visions were not some supernatural means of communication? Whatever it was, it added to the general strain.

I stepped on the bathroom scales one day and discovered I had lost twenty pounds in weight, although I have to concede that this new gauntness had an aesthetic quality that fitted people's concept of a faith healer, and the second and third public meetings went off well. We were getting bigger attendances, and consequently greater financial support.

But the pressures became still more intense. I was beginning to look at things from the eyes of Mark Kingdom, despite a vague consciousness that in reality such a person did not exist. The truth is that I didn't know whether I was coming or going. At one stage I even accused Doug of fiddling the books. He was shocked, of course, and when he threatened to leave, I realized I'd be lost without him.

Just about that time Magda came back, to see if I needed her help. She'd been working in Paris, so news about me was sporadic, but she'd heard some cock-and-bull story from George Kester and his wife that made her fear for my sanity. I was punch-drunk enough at that stage to have done anything—perhaps even to have gone back to Paris with her—but Magda was basically too decent to pressure me. In fact, all the incident succeeded in doing was to clarify my plans for the future.

I'd been talking to her about the meetings, and she was perceptive enough to realize that I had come to enjoy them. And that made me suddenly realize what it was—the freedom from involvement. With a stage between us, I did not have to worry about individuals . . . dying on me, trying to seduce me . . . even merely depending on me. My earlier fears about insincerity no longer worried me, since Doug was constantly going on about what the people wanted. "No more phony than being a politician or a pop singer," he used to say.

And that's really *it* . . . except for the day of Jessica's death; I don't honestly know whether I killed her. I hope not, but I must admit the thought crossed my mind a couple of times in recent weeks, when she was being particularly difficult. After all, if God had entrusted me with the power to reward her by bringing her legs back to life, who can say that I did not have the right to *punish* her on his behalf? But obviously I wouldn't have entertained thoughts like that in the cold light of day.

My reaction to Ingham's story was confusion. He looked defeated, his spirit undoubtedly having taken something of a battering, yet there was still a strong element of integrity about him. But was I being misled by the pleasantly normal atmosphere of Laura's flat, and the obvious sympathy of the two women? Could one trust a word like "integrity" when applied to a man who practiced as a faith healer, or confidence trickster, or whatever he was? He did not strike me as a likely murderer, but then how does one identify the dormant killer streak?

Come to think of it, what chance did I ever have of finding out? Not only that answer, but everything connected with the murder. I would have to speak to other people involved in his life before attempting to draw any conclusions. Meanwhile, I could not justify concealing his whereabouts from the police any longer, so I called Hugh Barraclough, the *Chronicle*'s lawyer, and got him to come to the flat so that he could brief Ingham on his legal rights. Later, while he accompanied him to St. John's Wood police station, I tried to comfort the distraught Norah.

Surprisingly, Laura's sympathies were more for Ingham than Norah. "She complains about others *using* him, but she's no different."

"Seems the other way about to me," I protested. "He takes everything, and gives precious little in return. . . ."

"I don't know the answer," Laura added, "but there could be something significant in Bill's relationship with women . . . all that stress is caused by something."

I dreamed about them all that night, as though I subconsciously expected to come up with the solution and the name of the murderer. But next morning, as you can imagine, there was no sudden flash of illumination, and I was tired and depressed at the formidable task confronting me. Still reluctant to face the Seeleys, I decided to continue collecting background information.

Part of the morning was spent in the *Chronicle*'s newsroom trying to get a better feel for Ingham the reporter, chatting to former colleagues and the news editor, Joe Lestrange. I also went back to the library to study cuttings of some of the major stories Ingham had filed. For the afternoon I had made an appointment with Sir Robert Cheatle, the forensic psychiatrist, who might be briefed if Ingham was charged—assuming in those circumstances the *Chronicle* did not decide to drop him like a hot potato.

Sir Robert, a dapper little man in his sixties, quick and precise in his movements, with a benign but convincing smile that seldom left his lips, looked what he was—the sort of man one feels impelled to entrust with one's problems. Even I got the message merely shaking hands, and I was not a potential subject. In keeping with the times, he appeared regularly on television, an "anonymous" but recognizable expert on all the "popular" psychological problems afflicting mankind—anthropological to sociological—speaking with equal ease and authority on all, to the not infrequent indignation of his specialist colleagues. But for all his "show-biz" image, he was a shrewd and down-to-earth

psychiatrist, good enough to be the instinctive recommen-
dation of the *Chronicle*'s own staff doctor.

He was familiar with the few known facts, but I gave him
a summary of the account—albeit different versions—I had
of Ingham's deterioration—from uncomplicated normal
man to a walking case study with the apparent symptoms of
split personality, his hallucinations and climactic blackout
before the girl's death—and asked for his reaction.

He laughed. "Instant diagnosis is all right on television!
But the scale of fees I charge to rich customers like the
Chronicle doesn't warrant snap judgments."

I smiled at his honesty. "I don't know about huge fees.
All we're paying for at this stage is initial advice. Employ-
ing you to examine Bill Ingham is a separate matter," I explained. "I'm only concerned just now with broad issues.
Faced with a possible permutation of possibilities, what I've
got to decide within the next few days is which is the most
likely, so that the *Chronicle* can reach a decision about paying for his defense. If, for example, we decide he murdered
the girl in cold blood, we shall probably leave him to the
mercy of legal aid."

He nodded, apparently concentrating so hard that he was
staring at my lips as though ready to snap at the words as
they emerged.

"The sort of advice I need is: On what little I've been able
to tell you, could he be suffering from schizophrenia? And if
so, is it presumable the defense would have a reasonable
case—if he actually killed the girl?" I asked.

Sir Robert pursed his lips. "I'm sorry, Mr. Coll. All I can
say at this stage is: possibly. The truth is that it is near impossible to arrive at a diagnosis from secondhand, unprofes-
sional comment, no matter how intelligent or perceptive the
witnesses are. I think you can see that I'm not just hedging

my bets. After an examination I would be prepared to go
out on a limb, but to speculate now would be reckless. Very
little is known about schizophrenia. It's an illness that affects
about one per cent of the population—quite a lot of people—yet the money spent on research is peanuts."

He leaned forward and gesticulated. "Take something
that captures the public imagination, cancer or leukemia,
and they can raise millions—but no one seems to care a
damn about anything as unsavory as mental illness, or even
something as "ordinary" as back trouble. I don't know who
is worse—the patients or the doctors—it's *only* a backache,
everyone gets backache!"

"So you'd have to examine him first?" I asked.

"Of course. There are too many imponderables. Do you
know anything about schizophrenia?" When I shook my
head, he tried to explain. "In a nutshell, it's all to do with
'identity.' What happens is that a person tries to cope with
the unsureness of his own reality by fabricating an unreal
personality from behind which the vulnerable self cowers,
omnipotent in an ivory tower. Thus he manipulates his false
personality to fit the surroundings. It's only when the hostile world breaks down this defense and invades the hollow
at the center that he becomes recognizably ill to the ordinary
person.

"Let's come down to cases. . . . This explanation would
presuppose Ingham was using Mark Kingdom as a barrier
against the world because he felt inadequate. But surely
there is no evidence of any prior insecurity?" he asked.

"None; on the contrary. Although perhaps I didn't know
how to root it out. . . ?"

He laughed. "I think you're being modest. But that is
what I meant by needing to examine him myself. You see,
until I have a really detailed description of these so-called
hallucinations, I wouldn't dare comment on their cause. It's

not uncommon for schizophrenics to experience psychoses such as seeing the little people, or giants . . . or a whole network of paranoid delusions. But one can get similar effects from prolonged overdoses of amphetamines—which is also quite possible if he was taking stimulants to offset tension and strain. Did you ask him or the others whether he ever took Benzedrine, for example, in significantly large doses?"

I shook my head, feeling it should have been an obvious question and that I had slipped up, but his smile was warm, and he reached over to pat my arm. Incredibly, I felt suddenly reassured, reminding myself that it had been my idea, after all, to consult a psychiatrist.

"In fact, it is essential for us to find out whether he took drugs of any sort," he pointed out, regarding me soberly. "I appreciate it's not the sort of thing one asks a normal person—but we have to remember that Ingham was anything but normal. You see, Mr. Coll, these visions or hallucinations are to my knowledge uncommon in schizophrenia. The pictures you painted for me, admittedly secondhand, have the hallmarks of a hallucinatory drug. Features such as the intensification of color, auditory as well as visual hallucinations, are common effects of LSD, for example, but seldom identified with schizophrenia.

"The same applies to certain emotions. His friends presumably regarded his so-called conversations with God as ecstatic experiences. Yet we don't associate this type of illness with euphoria, although again it can be induced by drugs such as LSD."

I realized we were groping in the dark, and although I intended to find some of these answers in my next meeting with Ingham, it was essential that he be examined by Sir Robert Cheatle. I hoped Sir Stanley Drummond would not lose interest once he realized that Ingham might not be as innocent as I had led him to suppose.

6

Next day I decided to stop skirting the issues and come to terms with the first real unpleasantness of the assignment—to interview the Seeleys. I rang them early in the morning, and after some initial hesitation they agreed to see me an hour or so later. Having crossed the first bridge, I was still apprehensive, and by the time I arrived my stomach was distinctly unsettled. Interviewing the parents of a murdered girl would have been uncomfortable enough at any time. But the prospect of seeking their reaction to a suggestion that Jessica might have aggravated Ingham's mental stress by her demands, physical as well as psychological, was quite hair-raising. How does one ask an elderly, highly respectable couple if they could recognize Ingham's portrait of her—as a sexually frustrated bitch?

My reception could not have been dissimilar to that experienced by Ingham on his first visit; even the Seeleys' appearance fitted the image I had of them. Jessica's father was a distinguished-looking man of medium height, fine gray hair set off by a ruddy complexion, with soft blue eyes—almost classical features, completing a handsome package. He was dressed neatly in a light gray pinstripe suit, perhaps a decade or so behind the fashion, but on his spare frame it made a striking contribution to his elegance.

His wife was a short, shapeless woman of indeterminate years whose dark, lifeless hair and relatively unlined skin indicated an age probably less than one's initial guess. She could once have been beautiful, but the expression was soured, and dark eyes, which might then have been described as sultry, flickered snakelike at me with suspicion. Certainly a long-suffering woman . . . the type that attracts misfortune like a magnet. Even had I not been influenced by Ingham's description, my distaste would have been cemented as soon as she opened her mouth. "We don't have to speak to you," she began defensively. "Can't you let her rest in peace?"

I did not know how to cope with this woman, close to hysteria, and found it an effort of will not to capitulate and leave. But Mr. Seeley endeavored to reassure me, delicately making allowances for his wife's aggression, and suggested to her that the interview might be less painful if she were to occupy herself making a pot of tea. Much to my surprise, she went to the kitchen obediently, without another word.

The favorable impression I had of him was strengthened a moment later when he declared his wish to help. Having listened to my explanation of the assignment and apologies for the intrusion, he endeavored to set me at ease, expressing an affection for Kingdom as he knew him. "If that young man did this terrible thing—and I find that very difficult to accept—then he was not himself, and we must all accept some responsibility for the pressures that destroyed him," he maintained. "I was the one who persuaded him to devote his life to healing, with no thought of the strains to which he would be subjected."

I reassured him that Ingham did not in any way blame him for those pressures, and indeed had spoken of him with affection and respect. I also repeated Ingham's explanation for his flight from the scene of the murder. His eyes filled with tears and I was tempted to leap in quickly with my questions about Jessica's relationship with the healer, but Mrs. Seeley chose that moment to return with a trolley on which she had prepared tea, cake, and biscuits.

No one could complain about her lack of hospitality, yet she regarded me with such hostility that I felt I might choke on the biscuit I had accepted. I could sense that the veneer of self-control was very brittle and that I should give her personality shortcomings the benefit of the doubt. But even allowing for my prejudice, I was finding it difficult to reconcile the strain she must be enduring with the degree of hostility. Nothing would bring her daughter back to life. Why would she be *so* bitter toward the man who had, after all, cured Jessica's paralysis? Was it because she was naturally vindictive, or perhaps because she had something to hide—something she knew about her daughter's behavior that would bring disgrace to her memory or to her family? I dismissed the distracting thought and settled for my prejudice. But I knew I would have to tread warily, and be especially gentle with her.

In the circumstances I dressed my first questions in a sauce of platitudes, concentrating on the period of supreme happiness when Jessica discovered that life had returned to her legs. And after a flood of tears that left her calmer and slightly more agreeable, Mrs. Seeley was able to paint a picture of events in the household at that period. Her voice took on a note of reverence when she described the "miracle," and there was no doubt that she still believed Ingham (or Mark Kingdom, as she referred to him) possessed supernatural powers. Yet when I interjected to clarify this point, her face instantly hardened and she retorted: "I didn't say *whose* powers. . . ."

I must have looked at her blankly, but she did not elaborate, apart from an enigmatic smile that no doubt I was supposed to find full of meaning.

Realizing I would get more sense from Mr. Seeley, I turned my questions to the business arrangement he had concluded to promote the Mark Kingdom platform, and learned for the first time that there had been two other men involved—although their influence in the venture appeared to have been insignificant. "We knew that he had a gift for healing, and with my business experience and contacts, I felt we could provide sufficient financial support for him to devote all of his time to this effect," he explained. "But even before he had time to reach a decision, it was really taken from us by the overwhelming response to Jessica's story in the papers. It was just as though the floodgates had been opened. Letters with money came in their many hundreds to the London offices of all the papers that had carried the news, to this flat, and many just to 'Mark Kingdom, London'—which the post office with customary ingenuity managed to redirect.

"And this was before he had given up his job, so that if it hadn't been for volunteers like myself, and other friends, he could not have coped."

I asked about the degree of financial support, and he was typically frank. "Initially I was prepared to put up a sizable sum as a trust fund in Jessica's name, but paying the interest to him. Additional funds to launch a proper campaign I hoped to get from sympathizers, but I have to admit we were able to revise those plans because money poured in unsolicited. . . ."

"About how much?"

He thought for a second or two. "Nearly seven hundred pounds in the first week," he recounted. "After that, it trickled to next to nothing, but we realized the answer probably lay in getting people to donate funds at personal appearances, and so we got ourselves organized with that in mind."

"I understand that Ingham—or Kingdom, as you knew him—resisted this attempt, albeit well meaning, to commercialize on his powers," I said.

"Very much so," he admitted. "We recognized him as a proud yet humble man. Until then he had been obliged to earn a living by other means, but our hope was that if the Call came, he would recognize where his real duty lay. Yet even when he no longer had any doubts, there was still a reluctance to commit himself wholeheartedly. It was the fear, I suppose, of being carried along uncharted waters—hurtling at an ever-increasing speed toward the raging waterfall just around the next bend."

I had a mental picture of Ingham in the maelstrom, with every drowning yard missing a final opportunity to jump for safety, or the relative sanity of his previous existence. But this was because I knew his background—Seeley had not. I asked whether he had ever questioned Ingham.

"It never occurred to me. I knew him to be a good man. Of course, he had to tell us about his previous life when the papers got hold of the story of Jessica's cure, but I never knew it really started as a practical joke until after he gave himself up to the police. I went to see him at the police station yesterday and he told me everything, as though he wanted to purge his soul."

Mrs. Seeley laughed. "His *soul*? You should have asked him to bring her back," she said accusingly. "It's too late now."

The outburst startled me, but Mr. Seeley behaved as though his wife had been talking to herself. He continued to stare at me, waiting patiently for my next question, so I said that I would like to concentrate on the "business" side of the relationship. Although complying, he insisted that the word be used in its proper context. "It wasn't a *business* in that sense of the word, merely an arrangement to organize his affairs, to put things on a businesslike footing. There were so many loose ends—letters and money pouring in from all sides—he would have been overwhelmed without proper help.

"Even before we reached a formal agreement, I volunteered my services as a messenger, collecting mail from the less helpful depositories, for example, although most of the papers, needless to say, delivered their own bundles—usually in the company of a reporter and photographer. And we had to get another friend to come in—that was to his flat—to deal with visitors and thus to enable Mark to carry on with a reasonably normal routine.

"I take it you were happy with Mr. Leighton's appointment?" I asked.

He nodded. "'Happy' is perhaps not the right word, but I think he was very efficient. . . ."

"But you had reservations?"

"Not really. Just that he was always in such a hurry—wanting to run before we were really able to walk. He rather put my colleagues' backs up. . . ."

"Colleagues. . . ?"

"Chambers, my bank manager, and Thomson, a business associate. Very experienced, both of them, but Leighton kept on at Mark about the need for specialist expertise, so that eventually they began to feel and look like bumbling amateurs."

"He seems to be very good," I pointed out. "I'm surprised, though, that he didn't concentrate on the promotional side, and leave someone like Chambers to keep an eye on the finances . . . ?"

"Precisely. I'd hardly describe two or three of us at most as 'too many cooks,' but he was always critical of what he called 'decisions by committee.' In some respects he is probably right—a good executive officer can act more quickly and efficiently. Besides, he came to us as a campaign manager, so there was no reason to suppose he couldn't do the job."

"Did you know that Ingham once suspected him of misappropriating funds? 'Fiddling' was the expression he used."

"Good Lord!" he said. The astonishment was genuine.

"I must say it wasn't substantiated. Ingham admitted being under stress when he made the accusation, and subsequently withdrew it."

"Neither of them said anything to me."

"Do you know where the books are kept?"

"Leighton would have them. Everything has been in limbo since Mark was arrested. Do you think I should get them back?"

I shrugged. "That isn't for me to say. Presumably you'll be having a meeting before long to wind up things . . . ?"

"I suppose so," he said disinterestedly. "There seems so little point in anything now."

I wanted to move on to Ingham's relationship with Jessica, but Mrs. Seeley, watching me in brooding silence, was a deterrent. She elected to say nothing, yet her presence inhibited me. Eventually I used the discovery of her daughter's body as a peg, suggesting that reopening recently healed wounds in this fashion might be upsetting to her, and that it would not be necessary for her to stay. Fortunately Mr. Seeley accepted the point, and persuaded her to leave us alone for a while. She looked at him reproachfully but said nothing, and noisily collected the crockery before stalking out. When she had gone, I went through the formality of asking how the body had been discovered, and he told me what I already knew—that he had gone into Jessica's room when she failed to answer his summons to the evening meal. He found her dead with blood all over her head, and a candlestick, presumably the murder weapon, on the floor nearby. He dialed 999 for an ambulance, but realized even before he put the phone down that his daughter was dead.

"Did you know then that Ingham had been with your daughter earlier?"

"I wasn't sure either way," he said. "Jessica was an independent girl, and her room was virtually a self-contained flat—especially when she became more mobile. We had our separate sitting rooms. People could come and go without disturbing us. . . ."

I was intrigued. "Do you mean to say that a stranger could have come up and gone into her room, without you knowing?"

"No, hardly a stranger. We would hear and answer the doorbell—unless someone was already with her, in which case they might come out to save us the trouble, assuming they knew it was for her. Sometimes, if she was expecting someone, she would answer the door herself—she'd propel her wheelchair into the hall, and then merely stand up to answer the door. She couldn't walk very far yet."

"Even so," I pointed out, "people—admittedly people she knew—coming and going almost at will puts a dif-

ferent complexion on the case. Did the police ask about
this. . . ?"

He nodded.

"What about other visitors that afternoon?" I asked.

"Leighton was in earlier."

"Leighton?! He never mentioned it to me. What time did
he arrive?"

"I don't know. We only heard him leave, but the doorbell
had rung an hour or so earlier and Jessica had called out to
say that she was answering it."

"Then what time did he leave?"

"About an hour or so before I found her dead."

"And how do you know she was still alive at that point?"

"We heard them both. She must have gone as far as her
door to watch him leave. He called out to us—he's always
very courteous—and we heard Jessica say good-bye to
him."

"She sounded all right?"

"Perfectly."

"Did you actually *see* her?"

"Yes and no. By the time I had opened my door into the
hallway, I saw the front door closing, and almost simultaneously Jessica shut her door."

"And you stayed in your room for the next hour . . . at
least, until you tried to call her?"

"Yes, between here and the kitchen. We watched television."

"Mr. Seeley, do you know what sort of relationship your
daughter had with Ingham?" I asked, mentally crossing my
fingers. But as I might have anticipated after such a tortuous
buildup, the reaction was a huge letdown; he did not get the
significance of the question.

It was pointless pressing the matter; the Seeleys obviously
did not see their daughter in the same light as Ingham.

I apologized for the intrusion on their grief, embarrassingly aware of my hypocrisy as I made soothing noises to Mrs. Seeley, and left. I was relieved that there had been no unpleasantness, but frustrated at losing the only likely theory I had—provocation. Had Ingham lied to me about the girl? Only he had the answers, and as I was shortly to discover, the police did not accept these answers, and would charge him with murder.

The trouble with television—news, documentary, or soap opera—is that it presents an image more imposing than life, so that reality often becomes something of an anti-climax. My first visit to a prison, for example, had none of the novelty one would expect, because I was immediately conscious of having seen it all before. I don't know whether subconsciously I expected an element of respect or even deference, but since my appointment was outside the normal visiting period—a special dispensation from the governor—it should have been obvious I was no ordinary friend or relation. And while I'm not unduly self-conscious, the sensation of being ignored can demoralize anyone. It was only after my briefcase had been searched and the documents perused with only a slight nod of acknowledgment that I realized one has to adjust one's values in the context of an alien society.

The relationship between institution, whether it be prison or hospital, and the individual is in any case less than comfortable. Over the years, old houses soak up atmosphere, storing characteristics of good or evil, happiness or despair, in some form of psychic aura. But institutions, monolithic and beyond human contact, remain indifferent to the dramas enacted within their walls. In life and death, the personality of the individual—prisoner or patient, officer or doctor—is reduced to insignificant proportions. I was merely a cog in the system, fulfilling a routine function interviewing another faceless prisoner—except that this prisoner was anything but faceless. Bill Ingham, charged with murder and now awaiting committal proceedings, was at that time possibly the most controversial figure in Britain.

Yet even Ingham, by reputation—or perhaps his own publicity—larger than life and regarded by thousands as a godlike figure, seemed overwhelmed by the surroundings. When I arrived, he was staring blankly out of the barred window at men exercising in the courtyard below. The noise of my entry made him turn slowly, and he regarded me vacantly for several moments. Yet some familiar quality in my voice obviously stirred the memory of our relationship, and the glazed expression was replaced by a faint smile. And when I inquired if he could remember any more about the night of the murder, he even attempted a weak joke: "I thought *you* had come to tell *me!*"

The optimistic note carried no conviction, yet there was no reproach in his voice. I did not know whether Ingham or Kingdom was in control, but whoever it was no longer believed in miracles. I felt I had to do something for his morale, so I said, "At least you look as though you care now."

He shrugged. "Perhaps that's not such a good thing," he replied. "I certainly feel more vulnerable."

"On the contrary," I argued. "The more interest you take in your predicament, the more we're likely to discover. Admittedly I've come up with nothing new, but there are a couple of loose ends which need closer examination and which might be directly relevant to your defense."

"Good! I'm all ears. . . ." He was suddenly alert, and I felt a surge of encouragement.

"Let's start with what I think could be a possible loophole

in the prosecution case. I'll have to take advice as to whether it is something I should follow through before the trial, or leave it to the defense counsel to handle. This question of access to Jessica's room. It appears feasible, although unlikely, that someone could have gone into her room without her parents' knowledge. . . ."

I waited for his reaction, but he had already anticipated the theory and his optimism was short-lived. "That would be too much of a coincidence, especially as I was with her all the time," he pointed out with a rueful smile.

I agreed reluctantly, but endeavored to dispel his pessimism by reminding him that everything still depended on how long he had been unconscious, and asked him what he considered had caused the blackout.

He shrugged again.

"You must have *thought* about it?" I pressed with what must have seemed impatience but what was in effect a manifestation of my helplessness. "You may not think you know, but at least you can speculate. Could it have been a blow—could someone have knocked you out?"

He shook his head.

"Was it another of your trances? Did you faint? Or, if there were any aftereffects, could it have been a stroke?"

He shook his head again. "I just don't know. The most likely possibility is that I fainted. . . ."

"From what cause?"

"Stress, presumably."

"Something between the two of you?" I could guess what his answer would be, and feared I was merely providing ammunition for the prosecution.

"She was going on as usual about our joint destiny," he recalled. "She couldn't understand why I did not divorce my wife and marry her. We had a strong spiritual bond, she said, and all she wanted was the opportunity to demonstrate how much she loved me . . . to prove that we could be right for each other physically—thanks to my healing powers."

"How often did she bring it up?"

"Practically every time we were alone."

"And how did you cope with that sort of harassment?"

"I dared not walk out on her because I was scared of what she might tell her parents. So I just tried to shut my eyes and ears and waited for her to stop. It must have been pressures of that sort—and there were others, too—building up that sparked off the hallucinations, so it wouldn't surprise me if I had fainted on this occasion."

"If you merely fainted, that would rule out any possibility of someone coming into the room while you were unconscious and killing Jessica. But if the blackout lasted longer, the proposition is not so farfetched."

He groaned. "It all looks so bloody hopeless."

I ignored the comment and asked if he had fainted before or since.

"Not that I'm aware of . . ."

"And what about the hallucinations—how often do they occur?"

He reflected for a moment. "Strangely enough, I haven't had one since Jessica's murder."

I was surprised. "How do you account for that?"

"I don't know. It must be because I've been cut off from the outside world. Nothing seems to matter." He seemed to anticipate my protest about the impending trial, and forestalled me. "All right, so I'm facing a murder charge—but that is at least a clearly defined problem, and the options are not mine. What used to get me down was the constant clash of interests between my two identities and their different sets of values. That's been resolved. There are no decisions for me to make anymore. My fate is in God's hands."

"But you do want to get off. You do care?"

"Of course. The difference is that it's no longer my responsibility; I can leave it to others."

"We're probably bringing in a psychiatrist to examine you in the next day or so. But when I mentioned the hallucinations, or whatever, he was a bit skeptical. Asked if you were on drugs. You didn't, by any chance, ever experiment with LSD?"

He shook his head. "I didn't have time for new experiences of that sort . . . too busy trying to cope with the one overriding Mark Kingdom experience."

"Not necessarily the hard stuff," I persisted. "He mentioned Benzedrine, for example. . . ?"

Ingham hesitated. "Before a meeting, perhaps. But nothing more than a couple or so, I swear."

I believed him, but I was still more inclined to trust in Sir Robert's instinct. "If you didn't kill Jessica—and let's assume you didn't—then the murderer was either an intruder, which seems highly unlikely, an unknown friend of Jessica's, which also seems doubtful in view of your presence, or from your own circle of friends and associates." He nodded, so I continued: "Let's deal with opportunity and motive. . . . Ruling out the Seeleys, the number-one suspect would be Doug Leighton. He was at the flat earlier. . . ."

Ingham shook his head. "Not Doug . . . that's out of the question."

"And more or less what he said about you," I retorted. "But the fact that you run a mutual-admiration society doesn't really cut much ice in a murder inquiry."

He laughed. "What possible motive could he have? At least I've already admitted to provocation. . . ."

"I don't know, of course. Perhaps he was trying to protect your interests. More particularly, there are several

things we don't know about Leighton. You admitted once
accusing him of fiddling the books. Why was that?"

"My nerves were especially bad at that time . . . wouldn't
have trusted my own mother," he said. "Besides, he gave
me a satisfactory answer and I apologized."

"But what actually happened?"

Ingham shrugged. "I happened to look at a bank statement one day and wondered why our credit seemed so low.
I was really talking out of turn because I had no idea of
what was going in and what was being withdrawn for expenses. I left that to the others."

"But you must have had a reason?"

"Only that a week or so before, Mr. Seeley had been
wading through a huge pile of correspondence, taking out
the postal orders and checks. He had got these stacked up
into two very precarious-looking piles and was warning us
not to cause any drafts in case they blew over, and he had to
start all over again. I remembered because it looked so impressive . . . must have been more than a hundred bits of
paper. But there was no apparent record of this input in the
statement. . . ."

"What was Leighton's explanation?" I asked.

"Apparently the larger individual items *were* listed, but
smaller amounts had been cashed for the petty-cash float.
He pointed out something I hadn't realized before—that
there were bank charges on all those tiny bits of paper being
processed, so it was much more efficient not to put them
through the account."

I made a mental note to check with my own bank manager, and asked if he knew where the books were. It was
obvious Ingham did not really know, although he guessed
that they were with Leighton. But why had the campaign
manager kept quiet about them?

By the time the warder had come back into the room and it was time to leave, I was pretty sure that if Leighton was not the murderer, then at least he knew far more than he had been prepared to admit. An educated guess was enough for me; unlike the police, I did not have to restrict myself to "admissible evidence." Once I was really convinced of his guilt, I was prepared to beat the truth out of him. Time was not on our side because of the increasing risk that Sir Stanley might withdraw the *Chronicle*'s support. I didn't fancy Ingham's chances with a conventional lawyer.

We shook hands, and although he showed no emotion, I felt a momentary quiver of excitement. For the first time since embarking on my investigation I began to feel hopeful. I had an identifiable target at last in Leighton, and I intended from now on to concentrate on stripping away the layers of bullshit.

Leaving, I was so engrossed in my plans for his downfall that I barely noticed the prison background or the men I passed on the way out until the front door, housed in the main gate, closed behind me. Only then did I come back to the present, reflecting how different my reaction on entering had been. Perhaps all that conjecture about old buildings soaking up atmosphere was a load of old rubbish. It seemed more likely that the people who lived and worked here acted like automatons simply because they were preoccupied. Heaven knows, they all had more than enough on their minds. . . .

The momentum generated by enthusiasm has a distressing habit of subsiding prematurely when it is not
supported by results, and I was soon frustrated by the time
spent on unrewarding inquiries into Leighton's background.
During my army days I gained considerable experience in
questioning suspects, but breaking down the network of lies
fabricated by a terrorist without resorting to force was in
comparison like an exciting game of cat and mouse. I was
now making very routine, even oblique, inquiries about
someone who might not have committed any crime—hand-
icapped by my inability to be specific and an anxiety that
my interest not yet be reported back to him—and the con-
sequence was that progress was at a snail's pace at a time
when I was impatient for results. And to make matters
worse, I knew I was becoming involved, which—as any
CID man will confirm—is hardly conducive to thor-
oughness in one's approach.

Having questioned the *Chronicle* staff who knew him, and contacts of contacts, I learned practically nothing new except a confirmation, if it was needed, that Leighton was rated highly for his promotional skills. Apart from the fact that he drank heavily, which was also hardly news, there were no known vices. He was neither a big spender, nor mean with his money, and was generally regarded as a pleasant-enough individual one seldom expected to cultivate socially at anything more than a superficial level. I was getting nowhere very fast until midafternoon, when the *Chronicle* librarian, Archie Jackson, rang me with a possible lead. Remembering that Leighton had briefly handled the affairs of a seven-piece American black soul group, the Sacramento Sinners, he had looked through the cuttings of the group's tour of the United Kingdom. Nobody had mentioned it because presumably it had not been considered relevant, but the cuttings revealed that the tour had nearly been cut short when one of the group was arrested on a drugs charge and deported. Fortunately for the Sinners, he had been a less important part of the backing group and a replacement was found, so that bookings could be met. Leighton as their spokesman in the UK was quoted at length in several newspaper reports throughout the affair. It was the central theme—drugs—that provided the tiny crumb of comfort I needed.

Chris Rayment, the music and show-business columnist, who had earlier shrugged off my interest in Leighton, was able to recall the incident, and to add a little background, although he was reluctant to associate Leighton too closely with the offense. "It's common practice for musicians, especially on a one-night-stand-type barnstorming tour, to rely on drugs to keep them going," he said. "There was no evidence they got the stuff here—in fact, they probably brought it over from the States as part of their essential equipment."

"But only one man was charged, apparently?"

Rayment shrugged. "Probably just unlucky, or perhaps he was the only one who used the hard stuff. Heroin is what they cited on the charge, so it's possible the police may have turned a blind eye to the weed, or any purple hearts and other amphetamines they may have found."

"But where would Leighton have fitted in?" I asked. "I'd be surprised if he was just the innocent spokesman. . . ."

He smiled. "What's your definition of 'innocent'? Probably different to mine. I don't think he was taking drugs, if that's what you mean, although I'm just as sure the group all were. But what manager doesn't know—and turn a blind eye—unless he's got a really long-term interest in keeping them healthy?"

I pointed out that while I was neither naive nor narrow-minded enough to condemn Leighton for being mercenary, it would be useful to find out the degree of his involvement. "Could he have *procured* for them, for example?" I asked. "Women perhaps, or even drugs if they ran short. . . ?"

He shrugged. "Leighton is the only one who can answer that. I'd say it was very likely, but you'll have to get it from the horse's mouth. Why is it so important?"

Having already told him about the paper's interest in Ingham, I was prepared to reveal a little more. "It's feasible that Ingham was drugged on certain occasions, without his knowledge. I can't explain now, but Leighton had the opportunity and probably the incentive. Would he know where to get his hands on different kinds of drugs?"

Rayment nodded. "It sounds farfetched, but—yes, he would."

My next step was to see Michael Williams, the medical

and science correspondent, but I was intercepted by a summons from Sir Stanley Drummond. To be strictly accurate,
his secretary asked if I could spare a few moments, but it
was common knowledge that Drummond was prone to
take umbrage at people who got their priorities muddled.
For a man of his considerable power, a man who did not
need to mince words, he was surprisingly devious. Unless
he was genuinely beside himself with rage, he was inclined
to cloak his complaints in the guise of pained confusion and
leave the actual punishment for the appropriate executive to
administer. His mother might have excused this basic lack
of honesty by suggesting that he was a softhearted man who
hated hurting people's feelings; certainly he was extremely
likable to those who did not fall foul of him. He was a tall
man, about six feet four, with a shy, almost apprehensive
expression—until he smiled, when his features lit up as ex-
pansively as those of Father Christmas. Drummond was
about sixty, but looked at least ten years younger.

It seemed that my apprehension had been justified. The
great man had lost interest in Bill Ingham. The murder—at
least, until the trial—was yesterday's news, and while the
Chronicle may have had an obligation to a former member
of its staff, it was an obligation that could be discharged
through the legal department. There was no need for my
continued involvement, and the expense entailed. He was,
of course, thinking of my welfare because he could not allow me to continue neglecting my shop. No matter how
worthy was my assistant, keeping a business ticking over
was no substitute for my own presence!

I did not have much of a leg to stand on, now that Ingham had been charged. "Another week or so would see me
finished," I protested tamely, "and then you'll have a comprehensive report. . . ."

He sucked in his breath with a pained expression. "Your conscientiousness does you credit, Matthew, but without the major story we were all hoping for, all I really need to know is: Does he *justify* our concern? Should we cough up for his defense?"

"I'm sure the answer is yes, you should," I replied.

His smile dazzled me. "Good man. That's settled, then. I don't need chapter and verse, so you can forget about a written report for the time being. Your judgment is good enough for me. Just pop along to Barraclough and pass it all over to him; his shoulders are broad enough."

With sinking heart I tried to stop the door closing on my investigation. It was not Charlie's wages that concerned me, but the *Chronicle*'s facilities that I would miss in going it completely alone. I protested that the police had a weak, purely circumstantial case, adding that I now had an interesting lead. But some of the hopelessness must have registered in my voice because Drummond nodded agreeably but was not really listening. But my last despairing gamble—the suggestion that I might save the *Chronicle* the enormous expense of courtroom representation—produced a more hopeful reaction. I was, after all, talking about many thousands of pounds.

"If I can *prove* Ingham was innocent and, better still, find the real murderer," I pointed out, desperately trying to transmit what little remained of my enthusiasm, "the *Chronicle* will not only save financially, but end up with a fantastic exclusive!"

The worried expression returned. Although I had introduced a fresh incentive, he was apprehensive now at what I might get up to. "You know I'm not concerned about upsetting the police," he said, probably meaning the very opposite, "but they're not fools. So if you know something they don't, you're treading on dangerous ground!"

I did not know whether he was being serious or merely trying to put pressure on me, because I was aware of the fact that his news staff would never think twice about concealing evidence when there was a story to be got—but then they were answerable to Herbert Mackay, who was a different animal from Drummond. The *Chronicle's* proprietor was fundamentally a politician who had worked hard and successfully at making friends with the Establishment—people he did not wish to upset for obvious reasons, unless the stakes were high enough, and an ex-reporter facing a criminal charge hardly came into that category.

"Don't worry," I assured him. "I intend to go to the police the moment I've got some proper evidence. At the moment I'm merely following up a strong hunch. . . ." I started to explain my theory, but he stopped me. He had more important matters on his mind, and the interview was at an end.

Mike Williams, the science correspondent, was my next call. I suppose it is only human to pidgeonhole people, to take one look and pass judgment. I'm no different from most. I have always pictured scientists as tall and thin to the point of emaciation—being too preoccupied with their work to bother with material considerations such as food. But Williams could not have been more different. He looked, in fact, like an adult Billy Bunter, which wasn't helped by his reputation of being something of a buffoon. Yet Mackay, the editor, employed only the best, and the fact that Mike had been with the *Chronicle* for ten years made nonsense of the gossip. The flippancy was probably a safety valve for the excess of energy that pushed him to the high standards of "popular science" journalism the *Chronicle* maintained. He was practically shaking with excitement when I had taken him into my confidence. Ingham was an ex-colleague, and *Chronicle* loyalty was legend. It did not hurt, of course, to imply that Drummond was backing my line of inquiry.

In his office, I repeated the gist of my meeting with Sir Robert Cheatle and the opinions expressed by Chris Rayment. What I needed to know from him was a little more about hallucinatory drugs such as LSD, and whether they could have been administered by Leighton without Ingham's knowledge.

He nodded. "No trouble. Probably a very likely answer, from what you've told me. It's usually taken on a sugar cube, and given the sort of access he must have had, he could have slipped it into food or drink anytime. The only problem would have been that it doesn't take immediate effect, so he would have to select times when he knew Ingham was going to be alone for a few hours. Another problem is that the effects wouldn't necessarily stop on cue—they could recur later."

I said that I would double-check with Ingham, and asked if the hallucinations described to me were consistent with "acid" addiction.

"Spot on," he agreed. "The short-term effects are heightened sensory perception—you might say an expansion of the consciousness—and these messages from God are not that uncommon. It's not easy to draw a line between what the experimenter calls a 'good' or a 'bad' experience—illusion, for example, sounds more attractive than delusion, and impaired coordination can be relegated to an unimportant part of a greater, more satisfying experience—but in itself it can be quite alarming."

"Are there any harmful effects?" I asked. "I mean, could there have been any danger in what he was doing. . . ? *Assuming* he was!"

He pulled a face. "Who knows? Personally, I doubt it.

LSD has a bit of a bogeyman reputation, and there's no shortage of scare stories, especially about suicide. But I think the consensus of opinion is that the drug is only likely to stimulate a paranoia already present. In other words, if Ingham suspected that his other self, Kingdom, was blessed with extraterrestrial powers, then the drug might confirm it for him . . . but equally it might have magnified any doubts and anxieties close to the surface. Leighton would have to watch the results of the first dose very carefully. If it achieved the desired effect, he would have felt safe in continuing."

"What about the danger of addiction?"

"Nobody gets hooked on LSD. You might even call it *anti*addictive. After a few days of repeated use, the effect vanishes and can't be reestablished even with a massive dose."

"You say 'massive.' That implies the risk of an overdose?"

Williams went to the bookcase at the side of his desk. "Genius though I undoubtedly am, let me check the facts," he declared, removing several books for reference. Sitting down again so that the chair rocked under his bulk, he pointed out that I had to disassociate LSD from heroin or morphine addiction, which frequently kill. He selected one of the books and leafed through the pages until he found the information he needed, at which point he uttered a triumphant snort and prepared to read aloud, prefixing the statement with a knowing aside. "Yes, this is it. . . . We were idly talking about 'acid' because people—including those who should know better—invariably refer to it as lysergic acid. It's nothing of the sort."

He began to read aloud: "The principal active alkaloid, mescaline, was isolated and synthesized as 3,4,5-trimethoxyphenyl–ethylamine in the 1920s. . . ." He looked up and explained, "What we're talking about is LSD-25, d–lysergic acid *diethylamide,* synthesized in 1938 by a chap called Hofman in Switzerland, although, strangely enough, its psychic properties were not noticed until 1943, when he accidentally sniffed up a few micrograms."

He skipped a few paragraphs, before continuing: "LSD is now the most powerful mind–affecting substance known. Twenty micrograms (one microgram equals one millionth gram) is enough to produce detectable effects, and amounts to about one seven hundred millionth of a man's weight. As powder this amount is almost invisible . . . but an even smaller amount reaches the brain. Even when the ordinary dose of between fifty and two hundred micrograms is taken, only two hundredths of a microgram is available in the brain, or less than one molecule of LSD to every three thousand cells.

"More surprisingly, even this small amount has left the brain within twenty minutes of taking the drug, while the effects of the dose do not begin in less than thirty minutes to one hour, and last from four hours to eight hours. It is supposed, therefore, that the hallucinogens act as triggers, releasing some body chemical that produces the celebrated psychic effects."

He stopped again and read silently, moving his head up and down, as though demonstrating his agreement. Finally he came to a reference he thought might interest me and continued: ". . . an interesting effect called synaesthesis: the transference of impressions from one sense to another. Thus LSD subjects can hear hands clapping as a shower of sparks, or feel a mild electric shock on the forearm as a bolt through the whole body. . . ." He looked up and said, "There are a couple of pages on the effects, but I think we can assume that the symptoms reported add up to LSD. The only real use for this checklist would be to go through it with Ingham. But the fact that he'll have experienced some, and not others, means nothing. It seems to me the best thing you can do now is to talk with Ingham again and, if what he describes points to the drug, then find some way of discovering how it was administered. . . ."

"Or *why*, if that's any easier," I replied.

Williams' eyes seemed to glitter behind the round lenses of his spectacles, and his whole body quivered with excitement. "Need any help?" he asked quite seriously.

I had a mental picture of Drummond's pained expression and shook my head. Promising to keep him informed of developments, I hurried out.

My recently acquired knowledge was still sketchy—
and, in any case, pure theory—because I had yet to
hear a firsthand account of an LSD "trip." I tried to rectify
this by applying for special dispensation to interview Ingham again in prison later in the day, but the request was
turned down by the governor. Despite quite unauthorized
pressure, the most he would concede was fifteen minutes on
the next day, but although I had to accept, I was not prepared to waste another twenty-four hours.

Leighton was the key to the mystery of Ingham's hallucinations, and if he had experimented with drugs on a
number of occasions, who was to say he had not been responsible for Ingham's blackout on the day of the murder? I
could think of two or three motives, but I still had no evidence, nor did I have any authority to interrogate Leighton
about those suspicions, unless he was prepared to be naïvely
cooperative—which was hardly likely. The more appealing

alternative was to search his flat for evidence of fraudulent misappropriation of campaign funds, or perhaps even drugs.

To guarantee having the flat to myself, I decided to trick him into a meeting in Fleet Street—a meeting at which I would mysteriously fail to appear. It was only midmorning, so I took a chance on his being at home, and was lucky. Having changed my attitude toward him so radically since our meeting, his pleasant voice on the telephone sounded incriminatingly smooth in expressing his "pleasant surprise" at my call. It was this professional pleasantness that made me feel, quite illogically, that I need have no compunction in lying to him. Afterward I was ashamed of the deceit— particularly underhand in the light of his circumstances—in the suggestion that we meet at the *Chronicle*'s offices to discuss some form of payment or commission I considered might be due to him for background information that could be classified as outside the brief of any story he was preparing for the *Sunday Record*. I said that I was going out of town the following day and wanted to get the matter cleared up before leaving. He was a little suspicious of the short notice, hesitating to commit himself, but in his kind of business it would be foolhardy to reject out of hand any proposition from a national newspaper.

Breaking and entering is another of the "talents" I had acquired in my military career, so the physical aspect of the operation would not be insurmountable. Since Leighton had a flat on the third floor of a block off Lissendon Gardens, Kentish Town, there was no question of gaining entry from outdoors, but I was confident I could utilize one of the "spare" keys I always kept with me to enter by the front door with dignity.

I waited at the corner of the road until Leighton came

out. Then I went up the stone stairs to Flat 6 and gave the
doorbell a perfunctory ring, not wanting the occupants of
Flat 5 across the hallway to overhear, my natural caution
preventing me from breaking in without double-checking
that the flat was empty. The door had two frosted-glass
panels, and it appeared from the gloom of the hall inside
that the assumption was valid. It may have seemed ridiculous to wait, since I had seen Leighton go out, but training
had conditioned me to follow certain procedures instinctively—and as it transpired, I was grateful for that indoc-
trination. I was already reaching into my pocket for the
keys when I froze—someone inside had emerged from a
room at the end of the hallway, and was coming to answer
the door.

The initial surprise was startling enough, but the figure's
long white gown or cloak presented a ghostly aura, and
after the shock my heart began to pound disconcertingly. I
was still slightly shaken when the door opened, barely
enough for the occupant—an attractive blond woman in her
thirties, dressed in a lacy white housecoat—to study me.
The face, full of character, was tense and the expression
hardly welcoming, but I suppose I was too relieved at
seeing living flesh and blood to bother about her manner.

"I've dropped by to see Doug Leighton," I announced,
wondering if I could have come to the wrong flat.

There was no mistake. "He's just gone out," she replied,
preparing to close the door, but I slipped my foot in the
way.

"It's very important—can I wait for him?"

She looked me up and down. "Are you a friend of his?"

I nodded and she seemed to relax imperceptibly, but not
enough to invite me in. "It's not convenient at the moment.
I've got company—you'll have to come back later."

I wondered what sort of company she was entertaining in a housecoat that was not designed for wear over clothes, but there was no question of coming back because—whoever she was—this woman could undoubtedly identify me later. I explained that I was passing through, could not wait long, and that in any case Doug had promised to leave something out for me if he happened to be called away. She regarded me suspiciously, demanding, "Leave it with whom?"

I was sure she could see right through my phony story, but I was forced to continue the bluff, and grinned sheepishly. "He was a bit vague about that, I'm afraid. He must have meant you!" I said.

She shook her head. "He never tells me anything, and I never go in his room, so I wouldn't know where to look."

My mind raced distractedly in an effort to relate her to Leighton. She was far too attractive to be a "platonic" flatmate, and far too offhand to be his mistress or wife—and, in any case, he had not mentioned any attachment. There was no alternative but to plunge in boldly and provoke an answer of some sort, so I asked, as charmingly as I could, if she could be Mrs. Leighton.

I don't know what reply I expected, but I was surprised when she nodded, although the way she qualified it seemed more in character. "You might say that . . . at least, we've been through a marriage ceremony."

I stood there like a lemon, feeling quite irrationally annoyed at Leighton's deception—tempting me to break in without knowing there might be someone at home! Then, to add to my bewilderment, she apparently had a change of heart, opening the door enough for me to enter.

"He's got his own room," she explained, "so you may as well look for whatever it is he's left. Let yourself out when you've finished." With that she opened one door for me and disappeared through another at the end of the passageway, leaving me stunned at my good fortune. This was a side to Leighton's character I could not have anticipated, since he had given me the impression he was very much a loner. The priority now was to search for anything else he might have reason to hide.

The room might have been a typical bachelor pad, the walls decorated with pop posters and photographs of himself with various celebrities. The atmosphere, when I switched on the light, conjured up a man at least ten or fifteen years younger than Leighton. One could imagine him bringing home a succession of young girls . . . until you remembered a wife on the premises—although, in view of her apparent disinterest, even that was still a possibility.

But the image I had formed from speaking to Leighton— the confident, even masterful executive on top of his job—was beginning to blur at the edges. How would such a dynamic character fit into this humdrum, incomplete, and obviously lonely existence, alongside a wife who obviously had little love or respect for him?

The room was used as an office, with a reasonably smart mahogany desk and small swivel chair by a window; a divan being the only evidence that he must sleep here too. Without any real indication of what I was looking for, I started on the desk drawers, wading sytematically through file after file of papers and documents without finding anything of significance. I read some of the old press releases with interest, confirming the general impression that he was good at his job, but until I arrived at the bottom drawer, which was locked, there was nothing to link him in any way with Mark Kingdom's affairs. A locked drawer was not in itself suspicious, possibly only a natural desire to ensure privacy, but I used a metal paper knife to force it open—and uncovered the secret to Leighton's financial affairs: bank statements, check stubs, paying-in books, and miscellaneous items. I glanced through them hopefully, but without more than a rudimentary grasp of accountancy they meant little. His bank balance was in the red—but only just—and there were no dramatic fluctuations. I was about to close the drawer when, jammed upright at the back, I found a large brown envelope full of postal orders; amounts varying from twenty-five pence to five pounds. Most of the orders were blank, although twenty or so were payable to Mark Kingdom. There was also a handful of uncrossed checks made out to Kingdom. I did not bother to calculate accurately the sum of what must have been several hundred separate orders, but a rough count gave the total in the region of five hundred pounds—not a fortune, but indicating a potential fraud of significant proportions, especially as (judging from the dates) other, earlier postal orders may already have been cashed.

What had Ingham said about suspecting him of fiddling the books? Leighton had acted indignant, and Ingham had backed down, convinced by what had been a reasonable explanation. Yet here was evidence that Leighton had, at the very least, been inefficient—and I was prepared to believe anything but that. The sum of money involved hardly seemed worth the intrigue, if one accepted his premise that the drawing power of Mark Kingdom was increasing by leaps and bounds. I was prepared now to confront him with this new development, but I needed to know more about his background—something he had overlooked during our meeting—and that meant another word with his wife.

I hesitated about disturbing Mrs. Leighton again, having little doubt she was entertaining a lover. But there was little time to spare, as Leighton might become suspicious—especially if he had something to hide—at my absence. Although the receptionist had been instructed to stall him for a short while, his logical course would be to return home as quickly as possible.

I listened, embarrassed, outside Mrs. Leighton's door for certain sounds, and when I was reasonably confident that they were not in the middle of the sex act, knocked somewhat timidly. There was a momentary silence and then a man's irritable groan, followed by her strained voice calling: "You can let *yourself* out, if you've finished. . . ." I flinched but could not back down now. "I'm sorry. I know it's a bloody cheek; I've got to talk to you before Doug gets back. It's very important. . . ."

"Christ!"

"Just five minutes . . . *please,* Mrs. Leighton."

"Later . . ."

"Without wishing to be rude, I'm sure that whatever you're doing can probably wait five or ten minutes. My business can't."

"Matter of life or death?" she retorted, disbelief in her cynical tone.

Before I could respond, the man's voice, heavy with irritation, interjected, promising her he would "sort out that nosy bastard." I heard what appeared to be the sound of him climbing out of bed and approaching the door, which he opened with a flourish. He was shorter than I, stockily built, and probably around twenty-eight, the sort of man who probably commanded a lot of respect in the local pub, having tried his hand in a roughhouse or two with some success. But few men carry much authority when they're undressed, and just now, very much out of his environment, he looked ridiculous. The manner didn't help as he

stared at me visibly bristling with indignation, and consciously working himself up into a lather. A naked beer-
swollen belly sagged over the waistband of trousers he had
hastily thrown on, and a cluster of sluglike toes protruded
from beneath flared bottoms.

"You heard the lady," he said menacingly, poking a
stubby finger at my midriff. His ill-concealed Cockney ac-
cent was hoarse, and I thought I detected a faint wheeze,
which did not augur well for his middle age. "I don't care
whether it's a matter of bloody life, bloody death, or your
bloody Aunt Fanny, we're *busy!* You wouldn't like it if I
was to come down your place and barge in—so you'll
understand why I've gotta ask you to piss off, won't
you?"

He was going through the challenge ritual, pawing at the
ground and making menacing noises, expecting me to ac-
knowledge his physical authority, although I guessed that
the ceremony was also designed to impress his woman as
well as reassure himself. Pride obviously meant a lot, and
although I had no wish to hurt him, I realized I'd get no
change from a slanging match.

There are many degrees of violence. I had studied them
all and no longer had to think about them, so I said nothing—merely smiling to disarm him. Then I lifted my right
shoe to lower it with accelerating force on his unprotected
toes. The pain must have been excruciating, and his eyes
immediately filled with tears, overwhelming his reflexes so
that he made only a halfhearted effort to swing a punch.

I did not even bother to lean away from it, increasing the
pressure, and shaking my head to emphasize the futility of
resistance. "Cool it," I instructed, keeping my voice soft,
almost intimate, before injecting a note of my own brand of
menace. "I don't want to really hurt you. . . ."

Demoralized, he looked at me with pain-dulled eyes; aggression replaced by fear as he waited for my next move. I instructed him to stay there while I had a word in private with Mrs. Leighton, motioning her to get out of bed and into her husband's room. She obeyed without a word and scurried past me, slipping on the housecoat as she passed but consciously giving me enough time to appreciate what it would conceal. Although her face was hard, with more than a line or two, her body was still eye-catchingly youthful. Aware of my instinctive interest, the man made a final effort to restore his reputation, threatening to kill me if I "tried anything."

I was already halfway down the passage but turned and stared him down. "Stay in that room, or I'll step on your head next time." He was impressed, and I felt ashamed at the way I had humiliated an unpleasant but otherwise innocent bystander. Reassuringly I added, "She'll be all right."

I had obviously risen in Mrs. Leighton's estimation. When I had closed the door and indicated a chair, she ignored my choice and selected another, a deep armchair that caused her housecoat to slip back when she crossed her legs, exposing at least ten inches of thigh.

"My," she purred. "Don't tell me Doug has been mixing with *men,* or was that a load of bull about being a friend?" I was still trying to decide my tack when she added, "You must be after him for something. . . ?"

I hedged. "Why would I be after him?"

"Nothing would surprise me," she said.

"You don't have a very high opinion of your husband," I suggested.

She did not reply, asking instead if I had a cigarette, and when I shook my head she got up, opened the door, and called, "Tony, let's have my cigarettes, luv. . . ." She leaned against the doorway, one hip thrust out like a caricature of Lauren Bacall in that marvelous film with Bogart, staring at me as she waited for a cigarette to arrive. And I don't mean that in a derogatory way because I regarded her maturity a damn sight more attractive than the actress at eighteen—it was just that everything about her was so exaggerated.

When Tony appeared he was dressed, except for his shoes and socks, and he had wrapped a wet washcloth around the foot that had taken most of my weight. I wondered whether any of the bones were broken and again regretted the degree of violence; it should have been possible to have subdued him without that. He glared at me defiantly, not completely beaten but recognizing wisdom as the greater part of valor. She took the cigarettes, accepted a light, and then, with a sweet smile, closed the door in his face. Then she returned to her seat, adjusted the housecoat more decorously, and smiled to complete the performance. Out of the blue, she dealt with my earlier question. "I wouldn't say that."

I had forgotten the point. "Say what. . . ?"

"That I don't have a high opinion of him. It depends. As a man, perhaps not . . . but the truth is, I don't give him much thought."

I decided to put my cards on the table. "Mrs. Leighton . . ."

"The name is June," she interrupted.

"I'm Matthew Coll. I'm a books——let's say I'm associated with the *Daily Chronicle*. June, did you know your husband was working for Mark Kingdom, the faith healer who has been charged with murder?"

She nodded. "He did say something about it."

"I'm carrying out what amounts to a private inquiry into the circumstances behind the murder. I seem to have un-

covered some sort of fiddle, apparently organized by Mr.
Leighton. Presumably that doesn't altogether surprise you,
from what you implied before. . . ?"

She frowned. "Will he get into trouble?"

"I'm not running to the police, if that's what you mean.
I'm only concerned with whether Mark Kingdom killed
that girl, and if he did—why."

Mrs. Leighton relaxed. "That's all right then. I tend to
overdo the act of indifference to Doug. I wouldn't want to
see him in trouble. He's got enough problems without
that. . . ."

"Such as what?" I asked.

"Just surviving. Didn't you know he's one of life's
losers?"

I was surprised. "He appears to be so much on top of his
job. Assuming that's a gross error of judgment, how does it
equate with him being a 'loser'?"

"It isn't easy for a stranger to recognize," she said.
"Doug *has* got talent, but he overreaches himself. If only
he'd recognize his limitations, and work within them, he'd
be at the top. He's been around for some time, and most
people seem to like him, so why do you think he never
seems to have more than one or two clients, and even then
only in the short term?"

I shook my head. "He runs out of steam?"

"No. If that were all, one of the agencies would grab him
to switch from assignment to assignment in tune with his
bursts of inspiration. The trouble is that he's not sufficiently
well adjusted to accept his shortcomings. He thinks it's
something to be ashamed of—so he continues to tackle
things beyond his capability, and falls flat on his face. Then
he'll pick himself up and do exactly the same thing all over
again, so that the chip . . . this monumental festering lack

of confidence, grows bigger and bigger. The only way he can (he thinks) put it into perspective for a while is by drinking. It's a vicious circle now because alcohol reduces his ability in areas where he doesn't need propping up."

"He *seems* so sure of himself," I protested.

"Of course. He's full of bull these days because he hopes that some of the confidence he imparts to others will rub off on himself—but they don't see him when he crawls back here."

"It's none of my business, but I don't suppose he gets much sympathy here. And *that* sort of thing . . ." I said, motioning in the direction of her bedroom and the man in there, ". . . can't do much for his confidence."

She smiled. "It *is* none of your business, but since you're providing the shoulder to cry on, I may as well finish. Doug and I have been married for fifteen years. It started going sour after five, and we stopped sleeping in the same bed soon after. I'm sure I don't have to explain that his confidence crisis also manifested itself in certain personal ways. It wasn't that which destroyed the marriage—I've got normal appetites but I could have managed, even if it had meant taking a discreet lover. It was his refusal to recognize what to me was so obvious. Any criticism from me—remember, I still loved him—was regarded as a slur on his manhood; any criticism from friends, as jealousy. He refused to change anything, refused to see a psychiatrist even. All he did was blame other people. . . ."

"How do you mean?" I asked.

She reflected for a moment. "There are dozens of examples. . . . He once handled publicity for a young pop singer on his way up then, although he's long since forgotten now. The impresario Robert Spink wanted to stage a concert with the lad topping the bill, but Doug was well in with the lad at the time, and reckoned he didn't need other people muscling in on his little gold mine, so he did the concert himself. But you need more than a flair for publicity to organize a concert on that scale—not least, a modicum of experience in business administration. It was a fiasco. Doug decided to hold it outdoors to get a bigger crowd, but forgot (or thought it too expensive) to take out insurance against the weather—and you can guess what happened. Only half the expected audience turned up, and most of those demanded their money back. Then there was a row because the box office couldn't cope, and there was no way of controlling the crowd. Instead of putting it down to his own inexperience, he blamed Mr. Spink for turning the other supporting groups against him, claiming the contracts had been rigged in some way at Spink's instigation."

"So presumably he's got a reputation for inconsistency?"

"In what they used to call 'show biz,' he's more or less finished," she replied. "I suppose he can still hold his head up in Fleet Street, and with the other media, because they only see the better side of him."

"I'm concerned with what appear to be his less endearing qualities," I said. "I'm pretty sure he's been misappropriating funds belonging to the Mark Kingdom Trust. Why would he do that?" I answered myself with another question. "Presumably because he needed the money. . . ?"

She laughed. "Who doesn't?"

"We don't usually go as far as to steal from our friends," I reminded her. "As I said, he gave me the impression he's the cat's whiskers, yet as soon as I step a bit closer, I discover he's a petty crook—'petty' being the operative word. Now, if I've understood you, he's a small-time Jekyll and Hyde, but I still can't understand how and why he made the transition from semifailure in his career and private life to crookedness. That's a jump, surely?"

"Is it? Most of us allow ourselves to be manipulated by circumstances, and Doug more than most. For as long as I remember, he gave up planning for the future. He lives for the present, and grabs what he can because he knows from experience that tomorrow it'll be gone. If I was a sociologist, I'd call it the 'fast-buck syndrome.' The Mark Kingdom situation is a classic example."

"He couldn't know the bubble was going to burst," I protested. "Must be the first time he's had a client charged with murder."

"No doubt, but something would have backfired—so his instinctive attitude would have been to take what he could, while he could. . . ."

"He claims he admires and respects Ingham."

"I don't doubt it."

"But robbery is a contradiction. . . ."

She shrugged. "He wouldn't see it that way. Ask him yourself."

"I will. He's probably on his way back now."

"Don't be too hard on him." She paused to light another cigarette and I studied her features in the glow of the lighter flame. Apart from their sensuality, there was character and hidden depth.

"You obviously still feel something for him," I said, probing. "I find that surprising, in view of the picture you've just painted."

She smiled. "Because I'm not bitter? I've been through that phase, but came to terms with it. Now we have a perfectly satisfactory landlady-tenant relationship, and he pays his rent—at least, most of the time—which is cheap for him, and supplements my income." She added, almost as an aside, "I run the makeup department at the Capital Television Studios. I'm there most days, if you ever want to reach me. . . ."

"I might do that. But since we're getting personal, who is Tony? I wouldn't want to step on his toes again, metaphorically speaking. . . !"

Her eyes wavered imperceptibly and the sophisticated exterior seemed to crack slightly. "Tony is a friend I call on from time to time for a specific service. Does that shock you?" I shook my head, and she added, "I don't sleep around."

June Leighton was intriguing enough, but it was her husband's background I had come to investigate, and I realized I was allowing myself to be sidetracked. I accepted her story, and the fact that Doug Leighton had conned Ingham and his associates, and me—but to what extent? When does a small-time crook graduate to bigger and better things . . . blackmail, perhaps . . . even murder?

Murder still seemed out of the question. From the character assessment provided by June Leighton, he did not seem capable of premeditated evil, and there was no evidence that he was a man of violence—perhaps the contrary. But blackmail could not be ruled out, and there was still the strong suspicion that he was in some way connected with Ingham's hallucinations. "Has Doug ever played around with drugs?" I asked.

She pursed her lips dubiously. "In the old days we smoked a little pot from time to time. Nothing else, as far as I know."

"But he seems to have been pretty secretive in other ways. Is it possible he could have experimented in private?"

"I doubt it," she answered. "I don't think Doug would have the nerve to try the hard stuff; nor do I think he's that stupid."

"Not even as an escape from his troubles?"

"No, not while he can afford his daily ration of Scotch."

I raised my eyebrows. "Presumably that's what the Mark Kingdom fiddle was paying for? Even so, how *does* he manage on the piddling income he must get?"

"Obviously very much from hand to mouth,'" she replied. "His fees are not much—probably just enough to pay the rent. I let him help himself to my food on condition he replaces what he can when he's got the cash. All the rest he gets from his photography."

While I knew Leighton did his own publicity pictures, I had not imagined it provided much scope for further income, but she corrected that impression. "He's built up a library of pop stars and groups, so that the magazines usually ring him first when they need a fresh print of someone in the news."

"His darkroom is here?" I asked.

She nodded. "What used to be a third bedroom along the corridor."

I made a mental note to look when I had finished with his own room. The fact that his estranged wife did not believe there were drugs on the premises was not enough; I had to see for myself, although even I doubted that he would have been naïve enough to have hidden anything incriminating in the flat now that Ingham was in prison. I smiled apologetically at June Leighton and started by pulling out the divan and looking inside the pillows and under the mattress. She got to her feet in some confusion and protested.

"That's going *too* far!" she said. "*I* wouldn't go through his personal things—and you're a total stranger. . . ."

I shrugged. "Sorry, but it's important. Don't let's quarrel over it."

"But I told you everything you need to know . . . and you found out about the money. Leave it there, please . . . or at least wait until he's back. . . ."

"Wouldn't that be even more humiliating for him?" I said.

At that point the telephone rang to stifle further protest. I knew instinctively that it must be Leighton checking up on me—and it was quickly confirmed by the way in which June Leighton took the call and dealt with his questions. Then, without another word, she passed the receiver to me.

There was no bonhomie in Leighton's voice this time, and I felt almost sorry for him when he asked what was going on. Making no effort to explain, I instructed him to get back to the flat immediately. "I've found the money you stole from Mark Kingdom. If I don't get your side of the story within the next half hour, I'm going to the police!" With the threat ringing in his ears, I replaced the receiver.

"He's coming back," I added somewhat gratuitously for June Leighton's benefit. "I may as well carry on. You can stay if you want . . . to make sure I don't plant anything."

She was upset, but I was already satisifed that Leighton was dishonest. Although I was not sure what I was looking for, I had a feeling there would be something hidden, so I ignored her and continued the search. After a while I became aware that she had left. For a moment I wondered whether she was trying to find a means of stopping me, but I doubted whether she would phone the police, or impose on Tony after what had already happened to him. I ransacked the room systematically, tidying up as I went, but after about fifteen minutes I had to admit defeat.

The darkroom took even less time because, although the jars and drums of processing chemicals might have been an ideal hiding place for LSD, I had no idea how to identify the drug. It was a frustrating experience, not helped by taunting memories of screen detectives dipping a finger into "suspect" powder and looking so incredibly smug as they instantly identified smuggled narcotics. I did think about trying it, but decided I did not relish the chance of testing the wrong thing—and having my tongue drop off.

It was even more infuriating a moment later when Leighton arrived as I was closing the darkroom door. His reaction could not have been more incriminating, and I was tempted to drag him into the little room and beat the truth out of him, but common sense prevailed. Instead, I returned to his room without comment, assuming he would follow me. Having heard the front door slam, June Leighton—who had dressed while I was in the darkroom—joined us, followed a few seconds later by a limping Tony, whose foot was still wrapped in a washcloth.

The men had obviously met before. Leighton gave him a perfunctory nod, but was too preoccupied to notice the injured foot. "Here, Doug, why don't we call the fuzz?" Tony appealed to him. "He's bloody dangerous!" He held up his foot for inspection, and I was so appalled by the swelling that I advised him to go to the hospital for an X ray.

"And what happens when they ask how it happened?" he threatened.

I smiled, "It was an accident. . . ."

Sharing my concern, June offered to run him up to the emergency room while Leighton and I sorted out our "private" business, and unhappily he accepted.

Leighton had said nothing, as though friends with freshly damaged toes were regular visitors, but I urged them to go. June Leighton went to fetch her car keys, and without another glance in our direction, or even a word to Tony, she opened the front door and left—taking it for granted he could negotiate the stairs on his own. Despite the state of his foot, Tony seemed reluctant to leave, and I could see he was racking his brains for a way of getting even with me. Finally, he appeared to concede defeat and walked out, limping heavily, and uttering vague threats half under his breath, although significantly he did not look in my direction. When the door had closed behind them, Leighton seemed relieved, presumably not appreciative of witnesses to his further humiliation. Some of the confidence returned. He removed his jacket and sat down behind his desk; *he* would conduct the interview.

"I see the morals of the *Chronicle*'s back-room boys are no higher than its editorial staff's," he began almost cheerfully.

I made no effort to suppress the smile. "You're a fine one to talk about morals—stealing from the hand that fed you!"

"I don't have to justify myself to you," he said without rancor, "but you'd never make the charge stick—you'd have to prove intent. . . ."

I shrugged. "I wouldn't quarrel about the dictionary definition, but in my book, stealing means taking for one's own use without right or leave. Neither Ingham nor Mr. Seeley know about the postal orders hidden in your desk drawer."

"Hidden?" He looked surprised. "You wouldn't expect me to keep them lying around?"

"No. They should be in the *bank* in Mark Kingdom's name. They were intended as donations to his campaign. . . ." I could see he was prepared to argue, and I pointed a warning finger, before continuing: "Don't bother to explain! I'm not the police, and I'm only concerned with one thing—protecting Bill Ingham's interests. So it's enough that I'm satisfied you were stealing. It's bound to color my attitude. . . ."

He was unruffled. "You're entitled to your opinion."

"Which is that you're greedy—but the question is: *how* greedy?" He began to look uneasy, and I took the oppor-

tunity to move closer, taking a seat on the edge of his desk
and leaning over him slightly, putting him at a psychological as well as physical disadvantage. My manner became in-
gratiatingly intimate—or offensive, depending on the
viewpoint. "No need to involve the police, but I've got to
know . . . if only to rule you out."

He swallowed nervously. "Got to know what. . . ?" He
struggled for composure and tried to get out of the chair,
but I pushed him back with deceptive gentleness, and he
made no further effort to move.

"Just how naughty you've been," I said. "For example, if
it was you who killed Jessica, then there's nothing I can do
to help. My first loyalty lies with Bill Ingham. . . ."

Desperation forced a reaction from him at last. "You're
mad! Why should I want to kill her?"

I shook my head. "Why should *anyone* want to kill a
sweet, innocent child?" I paused to allow a comment, but
he remained silent. "Anyway, Doug, don't let's quarrel
about it now—I may come back to it later, when I get some
more evidence. But if I drop that charge for a moment, will
you admit to something else. . . ?"

"I'll admit to nothing," he protested, reaching for the
telephone. "This is intimidation. I'm calling the police. . . ."

He started to dial, but I ignored him and continued: "For
example, being in possession of drugs . . ."

He faltered and stopped dialing. "What's that got to do
with this?"

I ignored him again, and maintained the same tack. "I
asked the police about your involvement with the Sacramento Sinners. . . ."

He was momentarily disconcerted and put the phone
down. The promptness of his action tempted me to try a

stab in the dark. "Seems there was some sort of cover-up. Everybody clean except some poor fall guy. Guess who the police think was really responsible?"

I think instinctively that my speculation was pretty close to the truth. He denied it, of course, but the protests were unconvincing, so I picked up the receiver and handed it to him. "Sorry, Doug, I interrupted you just as you were about to phone the police. . . ?"

He put it down again. "That's water under the bridge. It has nothing to do with your inquiry."

"Oh, but that's just what I was coming to. . . . When you told me about the hallucinations, I put two and two together and realized the effects you described must have been caused by LSD. . . ."

He tried to cover up his confusion with bluster. "We agreed the visions were all tied up with his split personality."

"Yes, in my ignorance of schizophrenia; I've since spoken to a psychiatrist."

Leighton wriggled desperately for a way out, but eventually he fell back on an apparent acceptance of my new theory. "Good Lord, that's incredible. . . !"

"Quite ingenious of you."

"Me?!" The surprise in his voice would have convinced most people, but I was beginning to dislike him too much to believe the truth.

"I *know* it was you," I replied, wishing I felt as confident as I sounded. "All I need is a sample of the stuff, and I was just going to start searching the darkroom when you arrived." The worried look returned, and I recalled the fear in his eyes when he first arrived and saw where I had been, so I added, "I don't know all that much about drugs, but I'll get the police in. The drug squad will know what to look for. . . ."

For a moment it looked as though he might be prepared to call my bluff, but when I picked up the receiver he capitulated. "We thought it would do him good," he said with a rush. "Get rid of some of the tension."

"Who is 'we'?" I inquired.

"Bill and I."

I lost my composure. "Is there no bloody end to your lies? You claim to have liked the man, yet you lied and cheated . . . and, for reasons of your own, introduced him to drugs—about the lowest thing you could do to a friend!"

"It wasn't like that," he protested.

"You mean you might have stopped when he became ill?"

"It's not like the drugs you mean. LSD is not habit-forming," he said. "It's not what you think . . . I wasn't really exploiting him. What happened was . . ."

I raised a hand to forestall him. "Some other time perhaps—I hadn't finished. I want to find out how far you went. As I said, lies, cheating, stealing, drugs, . . . what was the next step . . . blackmail?"

"No, I swear there was nothing else!"

"You swear? What difference is that supposed to make?"

Leighton was decidedly agitated. "I admit I lied before. You know how these things snowball. But I'm telling the truth now. I'm not a real crook."

The way he phrased that last sentence sounded almost pathetic, and sensing I was getting nearer the truth, I turned the screw a little tighter. "You seemed to have served a pretty good apprenticeship," I said. "Blackmail is not far removed from what you've already admitted, and murder is the logical progression. I'd put you at the top of the list of suspects."

Leighton was ashen-faced. "I told you—I'm not a crook! Not in the true sense of the word," he repeated weakly.

"What's the difference?" I demanded.

He shook his head warily. "I'm just a bag of wind . . . a bullshitter . . . which is why the lies come so easily. I might sail close to the wind occasionally, but if I step out of line, it's strictly small time. In fact, that sums me up: small time!"

I knew then that, by his standards, he was being honest at last, and I moved away from the desk to give him rather more breathing space. "What about a drink?" I suggested. "You look as though you need it."

He reacted gratefully, fetching a bottle of whiskey and two glasses from a well-stocked cupboard, and pouring us both generous helpings. He seemed to take it for granted that, like him, I did not add water, so I poured half of my measure back into the bottle. "I'm sorry I messed you about," he said, with apparent sincerity. "I really don't know anything about the way Jessica died."

"Maybe. But we haven't explained Bill Ingham's blackout. He thinks he may have fainted. Could it have been the effect, or delayed action, of some of the LSD he'd got under his belt?"

There was a momentary hesitation before he denied the possibility. "In any case, it wouldn't knock him out," he replied.

"So when was the last time you saw Ingham before he disappeared?"

"That morning?"

"And Jessica?"

Any hopes that he might deny seeing her earlier that day, after what Mr. Seeley had told me, were quickly dashed. "Early that afternoon," he admitted. "I didn't stay long."

"What did you talk about? Business, or was it just a social visit?"

"She'd asked me to take a few photographs."

"Did you?"

"Just a couple . . . head-and-shoulders stuff."

"And she was all right when you left?"

He smiled. "I can see her now. She was on top of the world—really pleased with herself."

While the latest discovery confirmed what I already suspected—that Ingham and his cause had been taken for a ride—it contributed nothing to proving his innocence. On the contrary, the theory that he had murdered Jessica while under the influence of LSD now seemed quite feasible. Admittedly the removal of the "intent" factor, if it could be proved, meant the murder charge would be reduced—probably to one of involuntary manslaughter—but I was not interested in the sort of compromise that would still deprive Ingham of his freedom for a number of years. My conscience would reject "convenient" solutions while there remained any chance of discovering what had really happened. Breaking through Leighton's web of lies had been encouraging; the final answer could not be far away.

Next day, in the afternoon, I had an appointment at the prison, so to occupy the morning effectively, I arranged to see Detective Chief Inspector Paget at St. John's Wood police station. The chief inspector made it clear he had little time for the "gentlemen" of Fleet Street, nor was there any sign of a thaw in the frosty manner when I pointed out I was not a reporter. Living well up to his reputation for being suspicious and unhelpful, he announced in clipped tones he was not in a position to discuss the "accused" with anyone except the accredited solicitor. His gaze went straight through me, and the sound level of his voice would have been more appropriate in a lecture hall. I toyed with the idea of mentioning my friendship with Detective Inspector Murdoch, but sensed it would not impress Paget.

Although I had come by appointment, it obviously did not occur to him to offer me a seat, taking it for granted I would not be staying. All that could be said for him was that he was at least consistent in his unpleasantness. I couldn't win; there was no question of discriminating against the *Chronicle* as such, despite the slight curl to his mouth when he mentioned the name, yet to have revealed my true identity would have labeled me as an amateur detective, which might have been even more offensive. However, the attitude was so unnecessarily rude that I could not help but react strongly, determined not to walk out, yet equally not to touch my forelock.

Fortunately I was saved from either course by spotting a framed photograph on the wall by his desk in which I recognized the military background and some of the people in the posed group. Distasteful though the realization was, it seemed we had something in common; the picture had been taken at Tadminster, the Army's special-services training college.

Even when I drew Paget's attention to the coincidence, the ingrained reserve prevented him from relaxing completely, although the sharpness of his stare may have been blunted imperceptibly by a glimmer of respect. Turning to study the group, he challenged me to identify any of the instructors, and only when I had proved I was not shooting a line did he unbend. It took several moments for the change to be apparent, but when he asked about my brief army career, the element of third degree in his normal tone had disappeared. We discovered that less than five years separated our respective periods at the college, although he had left the services just as I was going in and the photograph had been taken on a refresher course. After a few shared nostalgic anecdotes, he was a different person. He remembered his manners at last, pushing a chair in my direction and ordering coffee and biscuits.

Chief Inspector Paget represented impersonal officialdom at its worst, but as long as he was prepared to extend a helping hand I would make the effort to tolerate him—with the consolation what I could tell Drummond later about my "behind-the-scenes" sacrifices to improve relations with the *Chronicle* news-desk team, who had already complained about the good inspector. Putting the emphasis on *Chronicle* team spirit and loyalty, I explained my brief and what I hoped my investigations would reveal. He shook his head with more than a touch of sympathy for the burden that I had shouldered. "Take it from me, Mr. Coll," he said, "you're wasting your time. His only possible defense is temporary insanity. Broadmoor is full of people like him."

Wondering how best to draw him out, I decided to try the simplest way—honesty. "I respect your experience, Chief Inspector, and I wouldn't question your judgment. But isn't the evidence all circumstantial?"

He nodded agreeably. "Isn't that what we pray for? At my age I'm always grateful for such small mercies. Only in films do the police arrest a villain who might actually have been caught in the act of murder, when along comes some smart private detective to prove it was a case of mistaken identity! It doesn't happen in real life, as you should know from your training. Ingham panicked and went to ground because he suddenly realized the enormity of his crime."

"But what real *evidence* have you got? There's no motive, no witnesses, no fingerprints . . . nothing!"

He looked at me guardedly. "I've already said more than I should, Mr. Coll. I'm not prepared to talk about evidence."

I apologized. "Can I just clarify a couple of points *not* related to evidence?" When he said nothing, I continued, "I'm looking for other possibilities, other people, other motives. Ingham wasn't the only person who called that day. . . ."

"That's correct. We've interviewed three others, all of whom have been eliminated from our inquiries."

My heart sank. I thought I had been astute in identifying one—Leighton. He shook his head with a smile when I asked if he would tell me who they were. There was a limit to how far he would bend the rules.

I had decided against mentioning the theft of Mark Kingdom funds—it only complicated the issue. However, the LSD was very relevant. There was no need to be specific or to involve Leighton at this stage, merely to suggest the implication of mind-bending drugs. "Did you know Ingham's so-called visions were induced by LSD?" I asked.

"Are you asking me, or telling me?" he replied.

"Telling you."

The smile was cold but not antagonistic. Paget was pretty sure of his ground. "The psychiatrists will have to battle it out in court. I'm satisfied with the opinion of the expert we've consulted."

There was little more I could hope to get from the chief inspector. His mind was made up. I thanked him for his assistance, politely declined an unprecedented offer of an inspection of the police station, and had a pub lunch to revive my flagging spirits before going on to see Ingham again. The faith healer listened in silence to the story of my meeting with Leighton, finally throwing his hands up in exasperation. "It doesn't seem feasible I could have been so stupid," he said, pacing up and down in the tiny interview room.

"Your mind was on other things," I suggested.

He laughed. "I've had time to reflect since I've been in here . . . about power; what it is. I assumed—or rather, others assumed and finally made *me* believe—that my power came from God . . . or from some extraterrestrial source. But what is power? It's *energy,* and the way to tap energy is concentration on one course, to the exclusion of everything else. That's how millionaires make it; that's how the prize-winning scientists make it; that's how *I* performed miracles. Total concentration and single-mindedness.

"But I made the mistake of assuming that others shared the same single-mindedness. They didn't. Doug certainly didn't. He seemed to have spent most of the time feathering his own nest."

"Give him the benefit of the doubt and say 'some of the time,'" I remarked. "But from what I've told you, is it fair to claim that the hallucinations coincided with visits from Leighton?"

He thought for a moment and nodded. "And always when I had no appointments planned, so that he knew I'd be alone."

I had intended to ask him to describe one of the visions, but there seemed little point now, since I was satisfied beyond reasonable doubt what had caused them. Instead, I asked again about the blackout preceding the murder. "Leighton claims it couldn't have been LSD . . . are you absolutely sure you can't recapture a single moment in the period before or after. . . ?"

He shook his head. "No, I've tried. I've thought about little else. *After* I recovered presents no problem—I told you about that. It's *before* . . . all I can remember is the argument. Perhaps I should say 'monologue,' because it was entirely one-sided. I remember getting hot under the collar and dizzy, which I felt must be tension."

"But you didn't attack her at that point?"

"That's what I can't be sure about."

"You explained how you were feeling, but what did you actually see? What was she doing?"

"Doing? Nothing really. She seemed to be smiling. On reflection, I suppose that was rather surprising, since she'd been deadly serious for the previous quarter of an hour. . . ."

"Actually smiling?"

"Yes."

I tried to picture the scene, and it perturbed me. Why should her mood have suddenly changed? "Doug Leighton also said she was smiling," I recalled. "Or, 'very pleased with herself' when he left earlier."

"Doug?"

"Yes, he had been taking some photographs."

His face suddenly became animated as an image clicked into place. "Yes, of course! I saw one of his arc lamps in the room . . . those small, powerful lights on collapsible stands."

Leighton said he had finished and gone by the time Ingham arrived. Why would he have left any part of his equipment? When I put the question to Ingham, he shrugged his shoulders. It had not occurred to him before, nor did the significance bother him—the implication that Leighton had been at the scene of the murder at roughly the same time as he, something the police did not know.

I could not wait to find out. I phoned Leighton's home number from a call box, putting the receiver down when he answered. Now that I knew he was at home, I would catch him unprepared. I did. He answered the front door—June presumably was at work—looking distinctly unhappy at seeing me again so soon. He stood transfixed for so long that I pushed past him and went to his room. There was paper in his typewriter, and next to it the inevitable glass of whiskey—indications that he had been working. Dispensing with etiquette, I satisfied my curiosity and discovered an article he was preparing for the *Sunday Record*. As he entered the room I pulled the paper out of the machine and asked if he had a deadline. "This is a bit dated now—you'd better start rewriting . . . your confession in the first person." He looked at me blankly, and I continued, "I've just come from the police. Seems I owe them an apology; they're not as stupid as I thought. There were no fingerprints on the murder weapon, as you know—somebody cleverly wiped them off—but I made them check the door handle. And guess whose fingerprints they found?"

He was shaken, but not yet bereft of his common sense. "If you mean mine—so what? I was in and out of that room in the past few months."

"But they were the *only* fingerprints, or at least they were on top of any others, which means that you were the last person to leave that room."

"Impossible. Bill must have used that door handle when he recovered consciousness."

I chose to ignore the validity of his answer and said, "But you lied about leaving earlier—you were there at the same time as Ingham. He noticed your lamps."

"I forgot to take them."

"You *forgot*? You, a professional? In any case, they're not there now. When did you collect them? You haven't been back since the murder."

He had lost his color. Becoming increasingly agitated by the second, he went to the drinks cabinet and helped himself to a large Scotch, but as he raised the glass I grabbed his wrist and twisted until most of the alcohol spilled over. He made no effort to resist and I put the glass, with what remained of the whiskey, back on the desk. I had decided in the car not to resort to violence, but preventing him from fortifying himself with Dutch courage was hardly the same.

"What were you really doing there?" I insisted.

Without his liquid support, Leighton was noticeably cracking at the edges. He shook his head. "I took some pictures; I *told* you."

"I want to see them—show me."

"They're not here—when I heard she was dead, there was no point, so I turned the negatives over to the *Sunday Record*. The print they used ten days ago was mine; you can check that easily enough."

I was sure I could, but that did not make me believe his story. I moved in the direction of the darkroom. "Come on, we're going through that place with a toothcomb."

He made no move and looked nervously from me to the remaining whiskey in his glass. I emptied it on the carpet. He said nothing, seeming to disintegrate, standing on the same spot and looking vacantly at his feet.

"Come on," I ordered, and when he did not react, I grabbed his arm and pulled. To my consternation, Leighton collapsed in a heap, squatting inertly on the floor like a rag doll. I crouched down next to him, put my face close to his, and gently asked what was the matter.

With an effort, it seemed, he pulled himself together sufficiently to lift his head and look at me. The eyes were exhausted, and whether he found the effort too much or was too ashamed to look me in the eye I don't know, but the gaze quickly returned to the floor. His next words, in a near whisper, explained it all. "They were pornographic."

"The pictures of Jessica?"

"She made me do it," he added in a monotone. His attitude confused me—I was pleased at this revealing admission, but scared I might have pushed him too near the borderline of a breakdown. I took the glass and bottle of whiskey and poured him the sort of measure he might have taken himself. Even then he was too demoralized to respond, and I had to lift the glass to his mouth before, instinctively, he took over. He drank half without pausing for breath, and then extended an arm so that I could help him up. He made his way to an armchair and half collapsed into it, resting his head against the back and looking up at me exhaustedly. When he spoke, the voice was weak but calm. "I can't lie anymore. I'll come with you to the police if you like."

"First we've got to decide whether you killed the girl."

"No, I swear it. She was alive when I left."

"Then tell me what really happened."

He closed his eyes and appeared to put his memories in some sort of order. "When Bill discovered I had a little fiddle going, I managed to talk my way out of it, but I was scared old man Seeley and his friend Thomson might hear about it. We didn't have the same relationship, and they wouldn't have thought twice about getting rid of me, so I had to look round for a way of consolidating my position. . . ."

"And you thought of Jessica. . . ?"

"She was a powerful influence on her father. My track record was pretty good, but if I could use that as a springboard to really get into her good books, I felt I'd be safe. So I made that my policy. I'd always suspected she had a thing about Bill; there was no question of replacing him in her affections . . . I just wanted to be accepted as an integral part of the team, and a special friend to whom she could turn for advice."

"And presumably it worked. Before long she must have poured out her heart . . . about Bill. How he was blind to her love and saw her only as a patient. . . ."

"Exactly. At first I was just suitably sympathetic, but that didn't satisfy her, and she began to nag me to help her. I was supposed to be an ideas man, she said, surely I could think of something?"

"You really are a shit, Leighton! If that's the way you behave toward your friends, heaven help your enemies. . . ."

He finished the whiskey in his glass with a gulp and shrugged, unabashed. "What was so terrible about it? I was trying to help them both. You've jumped to the wrong conclusion about Jessica . . . she was intelligent, quite attractive, and even more important, she was rich. Anyone who married her wouldn't have to worry about money for the rest of his life."

My distaste for him returned. "That might be an important consideration to you—not Ingham. And presumably, if she didn't satisfy him physically, he could always manage with a bit on the side. . . ."

"What's so terrible about that?" he replied petulantly, reaching for the bottle of whiskey.

I took it from him. "You've had enough for now. Get back to the story . . . you were stuck for ideas; then what?"

The unfamiliar embarrassment returned. "That's where the photographs came in," he said vaguely, the voice trailing off.

"Go on!" I demanded. "I don't care *whose* idea it was . . . there isn't much to choose between the two of you, so what the hell! Just tell me what happened."

He was relieved at being able to escape the full responsibility. "Apparently he'd do anything to avoid upsetting her parents, so she wanted to exploit that Achilles heel in some way. If there were some pictures of them together . . . er, you know, *compromising* . . . sort of undressed . . . she could, well, she could . . ."

"Blackmail him into doing what she wanted. . . ?"

He nodded sheepishly.

"How did you do it?"

"I set up the gear, took a couple of ordinary portraits, and then hid behind the curtains just before he arrived. Jessica slipped him a knockout drop I got from one of my contacts. . . ." He broke off when he noticed my disgust, hastening to assure me there was nothing dangerous about the pill. "Nothing more powerful than an aspirin," he explained patiently. "Slip it in a drink and they pass out in a matter of minutes. Used to call it a Mickey Finn in the old days. Wouldn't hurt a baby. . . ."

He might have been talking about junior aspirins, his conscience completely clear. I cut him short. "So you faked the pictures while he was unconscious?"

"Why not? It didn't have to be Cecil Beaton standard. The only complication was that I had to shoot from behind, so that you wouldn't really see that his eyes were shut."

"You actually undressed him?"

"Yes, it was a bit of a struggle, but she helped me. All *she* had to do was to slip out of her blouse and bra. She used to wear a gold cross on a fine chain round her neck, and I expected her to take it off, but she didn't—deliberately, I think. Made it all seem a little obscene."

His matter-of-fact manner sickened me. Presumably, if it had not been for the cross, he would have seen nothing immoral in the situation. "Christ, Leighton, it wouldn't have made any difference to you if she'd been your own sister."

He looked indignant but it was only on the surface. "It's a job of work. I'm a professional . . . don't really *see* what I'm doing; only concerned about getting it right." He pondered for a moment. "Come to think of it, from the way she reacted I reckon she must have been getting a kick out of it—closest she ever got to doing it properly."

I was tempted to hit him but restrained the impulse, knowing I would feel ashamed of myself instantly. It would have been like punishing a child for something it did not realize was wrong. "Then what?"

"She helped me get him dressed. I got my camera and lights equipment together and left."

"What about Ingham?"

"He was still flat out on the floor, none the wiser."

"And Jessica?"

"As I told you yesterday—feeling very pleased with herself. Basking in the afterglow of the experience, or daydreaming about the hold she now had on Ingham, because she hadn't bothered to get dressed by the time I left."

"And that was in the normal way?"

"Not exactly. I had pretended to leave much earlier. Jessica had told her parents she wanted to rest, and did not want to be disturbed until Mark Kingdom arrived—and Bill had his own key, of course. We'd kept the door locked for the photo session, so I unlocked it quietly and crept out like a burglar. I had to get back to develop the negs and take the prints back to her—but when I did go back a couple of hours later, the place was crawling with police."

"That means we still only have your word you didn't kill her. And you know what I think your word is worth!"

"That's fair, but June was at the flat when I got back, and as I said, I'm prepared to make a statement to the police."

I spent a few minutes weighing the situation while he reached tentatively for the whiskey bottle. I made no effort to stop him this time. If Leighton was telling the truth—and now I believed he was—the time lapse between his departure and the discovery of the body was probably less than an hour. The chances of another person arriving by incredible coincidence during that short spell were remote, which meant the odds on Ingham being the murderer were shortened. He was the *only* suspect . . . apart, of course, from the Seeleys. I tried to dismiss the thought, but it was all too logical. Much as I dreaded the prospect, we would have to confront the girl's parents with the development. When I informed Leighton, he surprised me by agreeing somewhat apathetically, probably less concerned with moral issues than with the risk of criminal charges, and his promised statement to the police would be the greater ordeal.

Leighton had consumed half a bottle of whiskey, but apart from a slight film of perspiration on his face, it was difficult to detect. There were no outward signs; his speech was not impaired, and I realized he depended on alcohol in times of stress just as much as the sufferer from bronchitis needs his cough mixture. In the car he chatted quite amiably, as though he held nothing against me, and when we arrived he contrived to appear totally in command of the situation. He greeted the Seeleys effusively, as though nothing had happened, and introduced me in the manner of an ambassador.

The couple received us politely, and perhaps because I was accompanied by a familiar face, Mrs. Seeley was less suspicious than during our last meeting. We were offered tea, but I was too anxious to resolve the mystery that still remained to waste time on social ritual. Ignoring the sordid circumstances that were an integral part of it, I informed Mr. Seeley about the latest developments—that Bill Ingham had a witness for some of the time in question. "Mr. Leighton *saw* him faint," I explained. "He was still in the room at the time; not as we originally believed. But this proves, at least, there was no question of Ingham attacking your daughter *before* he collapsed, which had hitherto seemed the most likely theory. . . ."

Mr. Seeley nodded, but was obviously confused. "I don't understand. How d'you mean, he was still in the room?" He turned to Leighton. "We *heard* you leave. You called out to us!"

I felt embarrassed for Leighton, but had forgotten he was as slippery as an eel. He took the question in his stride. "You were meant to think that. Jessica and I were trying some sort of experiment with Bill, naturally without his knowledge—it wouldn't have worked otherwise. It's difficult to explain without going into a whole rigmarole, but I had to hide behind the curtain in her room, and act as a witness to certain issues that would be discussed."

The couple looked even more puzzled. "Witness?" the old man echoed.

Mrs. Seeley sucked in her breath disapprovingly. "You shouldn't have interfered with matters you don't understand. You should have called a priest. *They* know what to do—they're trained. . . ."

Leighton and I were equally confused, and although I recovered my senses sufficiently to ask what she meant, she looked at me with distrust and refused to elaborate. Her husband, visibly embarrassed, interrupted to put the ball back in Leighton's court, demanding a reason for the strange subterfuge, and what time he had left the room that afternoon.

"After he passed out," replied Leighton quite openly. "Since we didn't want him to know I was there, there seemed little point in spoiling all our plans by staying to revive him."

Mr. Seeley was stunned. "Do you mean you left him lying there? He might have been ill."

As I had discovered, Leighton was a natural liar, but tended to lose his composure under persistent pressure. He was distinctly unhappy about the tone of the older man's cross-examination, and his reply contained little signs of irritation. "It was obvious he'd just passed out—his breathing was quite normal, so was his color. We could *see* he was all right."

Seeley was not satisfied. "What was Jessica doing all this time? Even if *you* did not want to be seen by him, why didn't someone call me?"

Leighton was at a loss for words; I could literally see his mind go blank. For once I was able to sympathize—the truth was far too unpalatable for the old couple's ears. What excuse could he give on the spur of the moment?

I was about to intervene, suggesting that it was unimportant, when Mrs. Seeley burst in as incongruously as before. "She was bewitched." She looked at Leighton with contempt. "You should have known better—playing with fire. He was too powerful for you!" she exclaimed.

"*Who* was too powerful?" I interrupted.

She was confused by my ignorance, but when she saw that I was in earnest, she replied, "The devil, of course!"

Seeley intervened sharply. "She's been a little confused since Jessica's death," he said, stepping between us and putting an arm around her comfortingly. But she rounded on him furiously. "It was—I saw him!"

This time I was unable to dismiss her recollections as demented ramblings. I pressed her to say *when* she had seen him.

Mrs. Seeley, seeming to recognize in me an ally, regarded me with sudden interest. "Do you believe in the devil?"

I did not know what answer she expected, so I nodded cautiously.

"Dorothy! That's enough!" Seeley commanded his wife.

She did not, or chose not to, hear him; her preoccupation with the subject was obsessional. She came over and addressed me almost confidentially, as if she did not want anyone else to hear. "I saw the glow of him through the door. . . ."

My heart sank at such gibberish, but I had the feeling there was an element of reality mixed up with the fantasy. "You are sure?" I urged.

She nodded and was then lost in the recollection. "I didn't really know until it was too late," she said almost to herself. I nodded encouragingly, and she continued, "Ordinary people wouldn't, would they? Only a priest, perhaps."

I looked suitably impressed but said nothing, still undecided whether I should allow her to ramble on, but sufficiently conscious of Seeley's agitation to suspect she would eventually reveal something of significance.

"You see, it was a miracle . . . suddenly she could stand without support, and we knew that in time she would walk again. A miracle that we assumed was an act of God, with Mark Kingdom as the instrument."

At last it dawned on me what she was implying. All I had to do now was to persuade her to be a little more specific. "You were the only one to realize. . . ?" I said encouragingly.

I guessed what her answer might have been when she turned on her husband angrily. "*He* wouldn't listen! I begged him to stop Kingdom coming into our home, but he was bewitched like all the others."

Seeley was close to tears. He loved his wife. Her mind was unhinged, something he had learned to live with. Even Leighton looked embarrassed. A couple of times he had opened his mouth to interrupt, as though he wanted to bring us all back to sanity, but I suspect he was more than a little unnerved by the presence of madness, which, coupled with my own evident interest in her story, was enough to persuade him to keep quiet.

"When did you discover the truth, Mrs. Seeley?" I persisted.

The fixation about Kingdom was very real to her. She pondered very seriously for several seconds, anxious to be helpful. Eventually she admitted that she could not put a finger on a precise time or incident—it was, she said, the way Jessica had changed . . . the way she had cut herself off from old friends, alienated trusted friends like Father Taylor . . . her "blasphemy" . . .

Mr. Seeley asserted his authority at last. "Mr. Coll, surely we don't have to harass my wife anymore. You can see she's been under considerable strain. *Her* opinion of Mark Kingdom—the things she believes about him—is hardly relevant . . . any more than my feelings, which are very different, as you know. There's nothing to be gained from cross-examining her anymore now."

Incongruously, she seemed to agree with him, turning to me indignantly. "That's right! Why are you cross-examining me? Do you think I don't know the difference between right and wrong?"

I smiled at her sympathetically but addressed my reply to Mr. Seeley. "I'm sorry. The truth is more important. I've been convinced from the start, no doubt illogically, that Bill Ingham didn't kill your daughter. Sentiment is hardly evidence, but we've now heard—late in the day, admittedly—that he couldn't . . . at least not *before* fainting. The time gap between Leighton actually leaving and you finding her dead has been narrowed considerably—and even I have to admit it looks as though Ingham was the only one who had the opportunity . . . apart from you and your wife. If Mrs. Seeley saw someone—the devil or anyone else—we should know about it."

"But she *couldn't* have seen anyone," Leighton interceded. "She referred to some sort of psychic glow coming through the wall. . . ." Hedging his bets, he turned to her apologetically. "Even if that's what you saw, it's not acceptable in a court of law."

"But it wasn't just through the wall," she insisted. "It was so quiet in there, I took a chance on it being safe enough to open the door slightly, and looked in. Then I saw him lying on the floor."

"He was lying on the floor . . . the devil?" I suggested.

"Yes—he was asleep. I realized I was too late. My daughter had already become his handmaiden. She was almost naked. . . ."

"But alive?" I persisted.

The momentary animation in her voice faded, and her expression became pained. The memory was distressing, and it was an effort to bring herself to answer, so I had to prompt her. "Was she?"

"When I opened the door . . . only a crack because I was terrified, she looked up and laughed at me. I was so shocked I was rooted to the spot. It was like an orgy, except I couldn't see any alcohol or cigarettes, and of course there were only the two of them. But she seemed to be drunk . . . intoxicated with sensuality . . . because she ignored me."

The picture was pretty appalling, and I could visualize the enormous distress and shock this strange woman must have felt. Her reaction surely would have been unpredictable. I speculated on what it might have been, and asked, "You lost your temper—and hit her?"

She looked through me, dazed by the traumatic impact of the memory, and continued as though she had not heard the question. "I closed the door and tried to get away." The explanation was something of an anticlimax, and hard to swallow, yet she clarified the statement quite willingly. "I was *frightened* of her. She was always shouting at me to stop interfering in her life. . . . At times she seemed to hate me. . . . I suppose that must have been the devil's influence too."

"You mean you didn't actually go into the room with them?"

"I told you—I wanted to run away."

"Back to your husband?"

"No, I was upset, but I didn't want him to see her. I would have told him later, but I didn't want him to see her like that . . . she was horrible."

"So where did you go?"

"The only room I felt safe—the kitchen. I thought I'd occupy myself making some tea. As it happened, I made a cake too."

The matter-of-fact tone worried me. Either she was lying, or she was too dazed to remember what had actually happened. What a murder trial we had in prospect! Two principal witnesses totally confused and unreliable, a third a confirmed liar, and probably even more unreliable! "Where were you when your husband found the body?" I prompted, but she had another surprise in store.

"*I* found her," she admitted without hesitation. "She was my daughter. I couldn't stand by and give her up to the devil!"

Leighton and I looked at Mr. Seeley for help. It was apparent she could no longer distinguish between fact and fantasy, and at that point he seemed to throw in the towel. Placing a protective arm around his wife's shoulders, he admitted that they had concealed the truth, but now he was prepared to tell us the whole story.

"Dorothy had been out of the room for some time. I looked in the kitchen and saw that she had made a pot of tea, but there was no sign of her. I called and there was no reply, but the door to Jessica's room was open. I found my daughter lying on the floor with those terrible head injuries. There was no sign of Bill, but then he was the last person I would have expected to see—Dorothy hadn't yet told me what I was to discover later. My wife was standing just inside the door with the candlestick in her hand. You can imagine my reaction!

"I went to Jessica instinctively, but she was unconscious and only just alive, and I realized she would not even survive the journey to hospital, although naturally I went through the formality of dialing 999.

"My next thought was for my wife, although again I was really only going through the motions because she was completely shocked. In fact, in the few minutes I had attended to my daughter and phoned for the ambulance, she hadn't moved from the spot on which I'd first seen her, and was still holding the candlestick. I assumed the worst, of course—what else *could* I think?—but it was obvious she had no idea what had happened, so I did what any husband would have done in the circumstances. Jessica was beyond our help; the first consideration had to be to protect my wife. I pried the candlestick from her hand . . . and that was an effort because the fingers were locked . . . wiped the part she had handled, and dropped it on the floor next to where Jessica was lying. As I did so, I realized that she had stopped breathing. I checked her heart and pulse, but she was dead.

"My next recollection was an anxiety to cover the child up. She seemed so very young and innocent—the way she always looked in the old days. I couldn't leave her looking like a whore—but there wasn't time to dress her properly before the ambulance arrived. I just grabbed a dressing gown, slipped an arm into it, and closed it as best I could. The blouse and bra on the settee I threw into the wardrobe.

"When I heard the ambulance arrive downstairs, I had enough time to take Dorothy back to our own living room. I managed to persuade her to say she hadn't been out of the room except to make tea, and to leave all the talking to me. I doubt whether she really took it all in, but unfortunately nobody bothered to question her separately; I suppose they were being considerate. In any case, they were preoccupied at first with the murder weapon. There were no fingerprints, so the natural assumption was that she had been attacked by an intruder who had worn gloves. They wouldn't have given Mark Kingdom a second thought if he hadn't disappeared. As I said, not knowing what my wife had seen, I assumed he was at home and tried to contact him. I left various messages, but when he failed to show up, that man in charge pricked up his ears."

Mention of the police stirred me to action. Even then I hesitated before using the telephone. There was little satisfaction in knowing what I now knew. Mrs. Seeley's expression was puzzled, although she scarcely realized the significance of her husband's confession, but Seeley was another matter. The dejected slump to his shoulders told its own story, and even Leighton, with half an eye to the story he would eventually be writing for the *Sunday Record,* was visibly moved by the sight. He looked from Seeley to me, as though he were half expecting a shrug of my shoulders and an announcement that it was all water under the bridge, and that we should conveniently forget Seeley's story. I might have been tempted, had it not been for my obligation to Ingham. It took me only a second to decide—there was really no alternative. I picked up the telephone and dialed Inspector Paget's number.

10

It was only proper that every edition of the *Chronicle* should carry exclusive coverage of Ingham's release and the arrest of Mrs. Seeley, while the best its competitors could manage was a bare stop-press statement in the final London editions. The lead was so secure that even the evening newspapers could find little more to add, apart from a typically terse communiqué from Chief Inspector Paget.

The inspector, incidentally, had risen perceptibly in my esteem for the stoicism with which he had accepted the fresh evidence. The fact that in some circles it might be considered that he had erred in prematurely discounting other theories gave me little satisfaction. Paget had at least demonstrated that his interest was only in the facts, and if he had been wrong, he was not now ashamed to admit it.

My irritation was reserved instead for Sir Stanley Drummond, whose boisterous good humor at the satisfactory outcome to the investigation jarred on me. If I had re-

sponded to his sense of priorities, Ingham would still have
been in custody. That was all conveniently forgotten now in
the *Chronicle*'s hour of glory. At the same time, I realized
my attitude was unreasonable. It was not as though anyone
were attempting to steal my thunder. Drummond was quite
magnaminous. It was the limelight I was beginning to find
embarrassing, because in the cold light of day I doubted
whether my revelations would withstand close scrutiny. It
all sounded fine, but we had hardly attempted to analyze the
events with a critical eye.

When I got back to Laura's flat I phoned Norah, who was
so obviously delighted at the outcome that I turned in,
basking complacently in the reflected aura of the general
contentment. But my mind was too active for sleep, and
gradually doubts about the validity of our assumptions
pushed aside the remaining vestige of satisfaction.

Without a team of experts around me, I depended on
what people had told me. But was that enough? And while I
had little doubt at this stage that Mrs. Seeley had killed her
daughter, it was the degree of guilt that concerned me.
Jessica's life would not have been brought to a premature
end if Ingham had not introduced Mark Kingdom. And if
Mrs. Seeley had wielded the murder weapon, then justice
might now be served, but what sort of "justice" was it that
punished the innocent too? Mr. Seeley, for example, who—
thanks to my persistence—was now faced with a second
tragedy.

But Drummond's early evening reception to commemo-
rate the successful outcome of the *Chronicle*'s display of confidence in Ingham's innocence—very much the welcome
return of the prodigal son—was something of an ordeal,
exacerbated by the high spirits of the others. Apart from
key executives like Mackay and Barraclough, he had invited

close friends such as Norah Peters, while I had brought Laura. Ingham, to give him credit, was concerned about the Seeleys, but to add to my depression, I was becoming a little tired of his earnestness, his self-centeredness, albeit well intentioned. From the start he had gone his own way, brimming over with anguish at every crisis point, no doubt, but ultimately always doing what he wanted, and invariably with no thought for others.

When the executives left to attend to their duties, the conversation became more intimate. I knew that Drummond was prepared, in his currently magnaminous mood, to offer Ingham a job on the *Chronicle*. He had dropped a few hints about the publicity value of giving Ingham a column of his own, but he was astute enough to not rush his fences and allow the ex-reporter time to think. Ingham would need it. He was back to square one, with the headache of clashing interests. Although he had not really been discredited as a faith healer, it was unlikely that he would want to resurrect Mark Kingdom—the memories and associations would be too painful; yet he could not pretend that the past year had never happened. Drummond put out a few probes, but Ingham refused to be drawn, so he steered his way around the subject to fall back on safer ground, complimenting me yet again on my sterling detective work.

There was a chorus of agreement, apart from Laura, who gave my arm an affectionate squeeze, but I knew that talk of detective work in its traditional sense was nonsense. Whatever aptitude I might possess for deduction, for the application of logic and analysis, it had certainly never been exercised. I had accomplished it all by steamroller methods, by applying pressure to individuals until they had given ground or cracked. I was suddenly appalled by the realization that I might even have been accused of bullyboy tactics.

But an even more disturbing thought crossed my mind.
. . . I had blithely imagined myself battering down doors to
get at a "truth" that had been deliberately concealed . . . but
what truth? Did I now really have the whole picture—or
had it been distorted, knocked out of shape by the pressure I
had exerted?

Goodness knows how long I had been daydreaming, but I
was eventually brought back to reality by Drummond re-
peating a question about my obvious introspection. I must
have looked at him blankly, because he added with a degree
of exasperation, "After all this excitement I expect Matthew
is depressed at the prospect of adjusting to the snail's pace of
life in the country."

I was forced to smile at his single-mindedness. "I don't
mind admitting that in a way I miss the paper. I suppose the
grass is always greener . . ."

"Seems I'm not the only one with a Jekyll-and-Hyde personality," interjected Ingham. "You enjoy the tranquillity
of the book world, but miss the excitement. It was that part
of your character that I turned to for help. It was apparent
to me even though we had gone our separate ways."

He was wrong. He had turned to me because he was desperate enough to want to escape from London. But I was
not prepared to explain my philosophy of life; his assumptions irritated me.

"There's a satisfaction in books I can't explain, but for all
the so-called excitement, I've no real sense of achievement,"
I pointed out. "I suppose the only positive conclusion was
to get *you* off the hook." I regretted the rudeness until I saw
Drummond's smothered grin, encouraging me to continue.
"It was only a rather obstinate hunch that made me put
pressure on others. In the process I was contemptuous of
the police, for example, for relying entirely on circumstan-

tial evidence. Now I wonder if I'm not just as guilty in my attitude to Mrs. Seeley. It may seem pretty obvious to us, but she hasn't at any stage *confessed* to killing her daughter."

"Surely that's because she doesn't understand what we mean by 'kill,'" Norah suggested. "From what you've said, she relates it to a struggle between good and evil—Jessica being struck down by the wrath of God."

"Very likely," I conceded, "but since we are concerned with the law, did she—or did she not—actually *use* the candlestick Mr. Seeley found in her hand? I find it difficult to accept the supposition. Killing her own daughter? Infanticide apart, it must be exceptionally rare!"

Drummond was not really sure just how serious I was, but my defense of Mrs. Seeley had wiped the smile off his face. "I don't understand," he protested. "One moment you were convinced of Bill's innocence—and it was you who managed to prove it—and the next you're casting doubt on Mrs. Seeley's guilt. What *are* you suggesting?"

The answer should have been that I did not know, but I was reluctant to admit it at that stage. I stalled, preferring to clarify a point. "To be strictly accurate, I didn't prove Bill's innocence. All I did was to provide the police with a better candidate—not necessarily the right one. The missing link is that we have never really sorted out exactly what happened when Bill recovered consciousness. The ideal solution would be for someone like Sir Robert Cheatle to question him under hypnosis or sodium pentothol, and try to break down those memory blocks. You'd have no objection, would you?" I asked, turning to Ingham.

He shook his head, but Drummond squashed the idea. "As far as I'm concerned, it's over. You did a good job; the *Chronicle* has done its duty by Bill Ingham, and now we have to clear the decks and get back to running a newspaper."

I agreed that the *Chronicle* had fulfilled its role, but pointed out that it didn't mean the police had an open-and-shut case. "They never gave the burglar theory a fair airing," I said, "so even leaving me out of it, I think the news desk has an obligation to ensure that Paget doesn't take the easy way out again."

"That's another matter," conceded Drummond, "although we'd have to be pretty sure of our ground."

Norah was displaying signs of uneasiness. She had been picking at an immaculate fingernail, and now it had broken off, although she was too agitated to care. "Surely there are so-called missing links in most murder inquiries. Apart from the murderer, the victim is the only person who could have testified. Sometimes we have to accept the fact that certain features may remain shrouded in mystery . . . books have been written on the subject."

"*Sometimes,* yes," I agreed. "There wouldn't be a market if it was commonplace. But I merely said that the ground hasn't yet really been thoroughly covered."

Ingham was also disturbed. "I thought the burglar theory was dismissed as being too much of a coincidence, and because of the limitations imposed by the time not accounted for."

I disagreed. "It was discounted prematurely because your disappearance made you a more likely suspect. If you had been a qualified medical practitioner, they might not have been as suspicious so quickly, but Paget doesn't go overboard on faith healers . . . or anything he doesn't regard as respectable. And your comment about coincidence doesn't impress me because truth is invariably stranger than fiction. Anyway, there's something else . . . that hasn't yet been revealed. I'm convinced that something was *taken* from that room."

The effect of my pronouncement was shattering. Their

mouths dropped almost in unison. It was Drummond who found his voice first, but he did not appear very convinced. "Surely the Seeleys would have reported anything stolen?" he argued.

"Not if they weren't aware of it. Leighton mentioned that when she undressed for the photo session, he noticed a gold cross round her neck. It stuck in his memory because he found the idea rather *obscene* . . . his description, not mine. But she wasn't wearing it later—at least Mr. Seeley didn't refer to it, so the implication is that it was stolen by an intruder who decided he might as well get a few pounds for his trouble, or it was torn off in the struggle by the murderer and is probably still lying concealed in one of those shag-carpets in Jessica's room."

"Have you told the police about this new theory?" demanded Drummond.

I shook my head. "And they are not likely to work it out because they didn't know about the photo session—yet. If only I could find that necklace! If it's gone, the burglar theory becomes a very real possibility."

"I think the poor girl should be left to rest in peace," asserted Norah, and Drummond nodded piously, but Ingham seemed to share my unease. "But if the cross had been torn off in a struggle, the police would have found it . . . they must have searched every inch of the room."

"Exactly. That's why the burglar theory and theft cannot be discounted," I remarked. "He or she seems to have had about twenty-five minutes to play with. . . ." I waited to see if anyone would query the estimate, and then continued, "You must have arrived shortly before three-thirty P.M., and were drugged almost at once. By the time Leighton and Jessica had partially undressed you, taken the pictures, and put your clothes back on, it would have been about three-fifty. In fact, Leighton confirmed leaving before four P.M., when, as near as I can work out with her husband, Mrs. Seeley got up to make tea and, as it turned out, found herself drawn to her daughter's living room. If we can believe Mrs. Seeley—and she is probably too unhinged to lie—presumably Jessica was alive at that point, and you were still unconscious. Mr. Seeley says it was just past four-twenty when he found his wife and daughter—and no sign of you. This implies two things: one, that you regained consciousness and left somewhere between four-oh-five and four-fifteen, give or take a minute; and two, that someone else could have been on the premises anytime after Leighton left and before Mrs. Seeley appeared on the scene a second time . . . which is twenty minutes—*twice* as long."

"That's still only guesswork," said Drummond. "But it is worth putting to the police."

"To hell with Paget," I announced. "This is my problem; the options are quite simple. Either I can turn up that necklace and link it to Mrs. Seeley, or it was stolen—in which case the police are better equipped to hunt down burglars."

Drummond sniffed irritably. "It's a free country, of course, but I think I've made my position clear. You're on your own now."

I shrugged. "I agree, the ball is in my court. But a lot hinges on that necklace. I intend to find it."

It was my intention to search Jessica's room, but there was no response to my telephone call, so I filled in the time by paying another visit to Sir Robert Cheatle. I hoped he would still see Bill Ingham now that—without a murder charge hanging over his head, and the *Chronicle* no longer footing the bill—the case might not be so rewarding. Fortunately, professional interest overcame other considerations; an appointment was arranged, and I was able to return to the flat.

When it seemed that my involvement in the case had come to an end, Laura had taken a couple of days' leave, and now I was tempted to squeeze in a short break; there was no reason, for example, why we should not take the opportunity to get out of town for the rest of the day. But I had not counted on her being out.

In fact, annoyingly, we had missed each other by little more than ten minutes, because she had thoughtfully added the time to a note she had left on the kitchen table. It read:

Jackpot time—at last!!! You had a call from Bill's wife, the mysterious Magda—how's that for exquisite timing?!! Seems she wanted to congratulate Bill on his lucky escape, and while she was at his place, she overheard him take a phone call from Norah. Needless to say, she didn't understand everything, but the gist was that Norah has Jessica's necklace—she has it hidden at work!!!

The message was for you, but I didn't know what time you'd get back, so I decided to take a look while the sanctimonious bitch is at lunch. Will ring if I strike gold!

Love
L

I smiled at her enthusiasm, wondering how she—unused to subterfuge—would react if confronted by Norah or any of the bindery staff. But I knew I need not worry—Laura could charm her way out of any awkward situation. Nevertheless, since she had only a few minutes' start, it seemed a little pointless waiting on tenterhooks at the flat, when I could be of some practical assistance. She had taken the initiative and it would not have been right to interfere, but in practical terms, by working together we could probably halve the search time. . . .

I was lucky enough to get a taxi immediately, and since there were no traffic snarl-ups, I even had visions of arriving first and enjoying her surprise. My heart skipped a beat at the mental picture. . . . I would have to resolve the stupid impasse over marriage . . . one day some lucky bastard would beat me to it.

It was with some disappointment that I recognized her burgundy-colored Porsche parked at a meter less than a hundred yards from the library, although, since the taxi dropped me outside the main entrance, I estimated she would still be only a few minutes ahead.

As I knew the library, I did not need to waste time asking directions to the bindery, but the main workroom was deserted, and there was no sign of Laura. It occurred to me she might have lost her way and been delayed. I called her name, and when there was no reply, I wandered into the adjoining room. Even as my eyes took in the unfamiliar surroundings, I experienced a split-second extrasensory glimpse of Death, and knew instinctively it was Laura slumped on the floor of that drying cabinet.

A dozen questions jostled for attention, but I was running before any of them could be resolved, my senses totally uncoordinated. The door handle refused to turn and I had to look for some sort of control mechanism among the row of knobs and switches on the cabinet's metal side. The only thing I really took in was the temperature-gauge reading of 49.5° C, which I knew instinctively was dangerously high. I controlled a roar of frustration as I tugged at the handle, and then a button on the handle moved, and the door swung open.

The heat that met me as I bent to pull Laura's unconscious form clear of the cabinet seemed to have the substance of a brick wall. Even in my overwrought state I tried to fathom why her sweater had been pulled up over her head, and pulling it back, I was alarmed by the vivid redness of her skin, almost as though she had fallen asleep in the sun. Then, as the other side of her back came into view, I was horrified to discover that a large strip of skin had actually disappeared, exposing the savagely burned flesh below. But even that stomach-turning sight was neutralized by enormous relief at the imperceptible quiver of her nostrils, which indicated that she was still breathing . . . just.

For a moment I panicked, uncertain of the priorities, whether to get her breathing properly, or get professional help. In the event my reaction was probably instinctive— grabbing the nearest phone and dialing 999.

By the time the ambulance arrived—it seemed an eternity, but I saw from my watch that it was barely three minutes—Laura was breathing more normally, and obviously regaining consciousness. I went with her to Middlesex Hospital, where, despite her protests that she had fully recovered, she was admitted.

The Nigerian doctor in emergency was more concerned with the burns—although fortunately they were restricted to one area—than her general ordeal, and, wondering inconsequentially whether coming from Africa automatically made him an authority on heat exposure, I controlled an urge to laugh hysterically.

Referring to the extent of the burns, he warned, "Don't be misled by the absence of pain—that's what the injection was for. In fact, you may need some long-term treatment, even a skin graft—but in the short term we're more concerned with the possibility of infection. Apart from that, you're as fit as a fiddle!"

He had not seen her, unconscious, in the cabinet, I protested. "I agree she looks all right now, but what about possible side effects? The temperature in that cabinet was way above one hundred degrees Fahrenheit when I pulled her out!" I'd had time to do the conversion from centigrade and the knowledge had terrified me, aware that normal body temperature is around ninety-eight degrees, and that people could die from fevers of just over a hundred.

"We might have kept her overnight apart from the burns," he acknowledged. "But there shouldn't be anything to worry about; recovery is usually very quick once the

brain's heat-control mechanism is functioning properly
again. . . ."

"What a time for it to pack up," Laura remarked, her
sense of humor fully restored. "When I needed it most . . ."

The doctor showed his white teeth in a smile. "It's not
geared for oven temperatures. The control mechanism
causes the body to sweat to get rid of heat in hot weather,
but like any normally efficient piece of equipment, it can
*over*heat if asked to do too much. Our task now is to rehy-
drate you. In fact, it wouldn't do any harm to put you on an
intravenous alkali drip for a few hours."

"How can I be hydrated? I didn't even sweat. . . ."

"Take it from me you did," he said. "You were misled
because it was too quick a process for normal perspiration—
it was *sucked* out, evaporating in one action. Indeed, it was
that which caused you to lose consciousness; something we
call periphery circulatory failure."

"What does that mean?" I asked.

"The blood is drawn to the surface of the skin until there
isn't enough left for the heart to circulate it properly. Another minute or so, and Miss Cottingham might never have
recovered. You most likely saved her life!"

Laura's eyes turned to me. "My hero! Just goes to prove I
was right to be polite to you—I knew you would come in
handy one of these days!"

Despite her cheerfulness she looked drained of energy,
and I announced that I was leaving so that she could get
some rest, but she detained me with a glance. "Thanks for
everything," she told the doctor. "I'm sorry to have been so
stupid."

When he had gone, she turned to me. "It wasn't an accident. That door didn't close of its own accord."

I had already reached the same conclusion. "I'm going

back to take another look. From what I remember, there were too many safety gadgets for an accident."

"Then perhaps we should tell the police?"

I wrinkled my nose. "Paget would say you had been infected by Ingham's hallucinations. From what *we* already know, if the helpless Miss Peters is behind this, it will be simple to link her with Jessica's murder."

"I'd like to give her a taste of her own medicine," Laura protested.

"Perhaps we'll do that anyway," I conceded, "but we'd have to be sure it was her. It may have been a trap, but not necessarily her who sprang it. . . ."

She stared at me. "I suppose I did charge in a bit blindly . . . but it must have been her."

I kissed her on each cheek and then gently on the lips. "It may have been a bit headstrong, but only in the best Coll tradition. We can be clever with hindsight, but what we both forgot at the time was that Magda Ingham is working in Paris—which is why I haven't bothered to see her. And if she did turn up last night and heard what she is supposed to have overheard, why should she realize its significance, and why would she ring me, of all people? Come to think of it, how do we even know it was her who rang?"

Laura pulled a face. "If someone rings with what seems like vital information, who would stop to query their identity? Would you?"

I shook my head.

But I did not get very far with Norah Peters. She seemed genuinely shocked at what had happened, and I had no evidence to support my suspicion.

"They told me when I got back from lunch," she explained. "They said it was a young woman, but there was no reason to suspect it was Laura. What on earth was she doing here?"

"Doesn't it strike you as significant that a once-in-a-million accident, if that's what you think it was, should happen to Laura, of all people—the one person involved with me in investigating Jessica Seeley's murder?"

She looked aghast. "You don't suspect *me*. . . ?"

"I must say that the possibility had crossed our minds," I said with heavy irony. "Laura intercepted a message intended for me. If someone was concerned enough about us finding the necklace, is it so unlikely that they would decide to get rid of us?"

"Get rid of? You can't imagine someone . . . me . . . tried to *kill* Laura! It's impossible!"

"You tell that to the ambulance people, or the doctor. Another minute, and she wouldn't have survived, he said."

"It can't be true," she protested. "It would have been a nightmare, I admit, but she wouldn't have died."

"The temperature gauge goes up to a hundred degrees centigrade . . . that's two hundred twelve degrees Fahrenheit. . . ."

"That's too high for our requirements; there's a cut-out device that operates at fifty-five degrees centigrade . . . and then there's a second . . ."

"It was touching fifty degrees when I got her out—she would have been dead long before the cut-out point! What about the second one?"

"The machine switches itself off after sixty minutes."

"That's nice to know," I retorted. "We estimate Laura was in that machine for twelve minutes, so all she had to do was to cross her fingers for another forty-eight minutes and everything would have been all right!"

"But if what you say is true, someone had to turn on the heat and fan. I wasn't even here. . . ."

"And I suppose someone will swear you were never out of their sight for the whole of the lunch period?"

"As a matter of fact, I was alone, but . . ."

I shrugged. I knew I was incapable of behaving dispassionately, and that whatever she said would not be taken at its face value. It was highly unlikely that by prolonging the interview I would cause her to break down and confess. It was not until later that it occurred to me that the switching mechanism might have been preset.

I returned to the hospital to put Laura in the picture and then came back to the flat to do some thinking. My mistake had been to wait for things to be handed to me on a plate, to react instead of taking the initiative. . . . One thing was certain: that Laura's misfortune had been no accident—which meant that the investigation was worrying someone. The awareness was enough to make me take a gamble. I made three telephone calls.

Sitting in complete darkness in Jessica's room that evening was an eerie experience. I had not been here before—discussions with the Seeleys having been conducted in their own living room—but her personality hovered in the atmosphere as heavily as perfume. Impressions of her had been gained only through the eyes of others, but after ten minutes alone in the room, I felt I could visualize her clearly for the first time. A surrealist painting in oils, half completed, confirmed my mental picture of a beauty blemished by a brooding, even evil presence.

I had begun by searching under the rugs and the carpet and under the settee and armchairs for the missing cross and chain, or any part of it, although, as I had anticipated, a vital piece of evidence would not have escaped the sharp eyes of the CID men, despite what I had intimated in Drummond's office. But I did find it eventually in her jewel box, the delicate chain snapped. Jessica would not have taken it off—if she had, it would not have been broken—which meant that someone had torn it off and returned it to the jewel box. Her father? I thought not. I put it in my pocket, switched off the light, and sat back to wait, putting my conviction to the test—that someone would come looking for it before I could speak to the police.

I chose a position somewhat instinctively behind the settee, until cramp, in whatever position I tried, forced me into an armchair. However, since I could not be seen from the door, I was able to relax and rethink the case, retracing my movements, lingering perhaps over the meeting with June Leighton, but endeavoring dispassionately to uncover some tiny clue I might have missed at the time. I had almost completed this memory cycle for the second time when the gloom and stillness of the room caused me to doze off.

It was the sharp click of a door closing that alerted me so I was sufficiently awake to remain still and listen. Someone was in the room. The silhouette was tall and gaunt, and although I could not discern the face, I guessed it was Ingham. He was standing uncertainly in the center of the room, looking at the carpet, although it was too dark for him to see anything; *not* looking, in fact, but watchful and waiting, as though he had come for a purpose, but had not yet remembered what it was.

I racked my brains for something impressive to say, but everything seemed hysterically funny rather than dramatic, so I kept quiet. But as I got out of the armchair, I held out the cross and asked if this was what he had been looking for.

The shock of seeing an apparition suddenly uncurl itself, and rise up in a dead girl's room, is enough to frighten anyone out of his wits, so Ingham's reaction was hardly surprising. Eyes riveted on the cross dangling from my fingers, he seemed to gasp for air as though fighting a mild seizure. But for the loss of air from his lungs, I think he would have screamed with terror. Then, as he stood, legs outstretched like a petrified scarecrow, currents of energy seemed to surge through his trembling limbs like a spring tide, until it finally washed over his brain—releasing an inhuman force irresistibly attracted to the cross and chain. At that moment I doubt whether he was conscious of me as a person or merely as an obstacle, and he crashed into me with the primeval power of a Dr. Who monster, so that I was suddenly fighting for my life.

I suppose it must have been the awesome glitter in his eyes that made me panic, forget my training, and get involved in a desperate brawling wrestling match in which I was at a disadvantage. Nothing is more unsettling in this sort of situation than an awareness of one's inadequacy, and my thinking became confused. Actions seemed to take on a dreamlike quality in which my movements were in cumbersome slow motion, while my opponent was sharp, vicious, and highly dangerous. In normal circumstances I would have dropped him before he got to close quarters, but now I was concerned primarily with protecting myself, all the time unhappily conscious of my labored breathing and clumsiness—like the nightmare where you try to beat off the bogeyman and watch your punches merely passing through it. Now I was resorting to roundhouse swings that were going round the back of his neck, while the effort and tension were making my arms feel like lead.

All the time he was searching for a hold on my throat, and ironically the thing that saved me was landing a clumsy swing on his ear, painful enough to stop his grappling and to make him take an instinctive punch at me. My reactions were sufficiently slow for the blow to catch me high up on the cheek, throwing me against the back of the settee, so that I overbalanced and somersaulted over the cushions to the floor. The momentum was so great that I landed on my feet again, and I had the distinct impression that the fight was not real . . . that it was a film, and we were stuntmen. But then the pain reverberated through my head, reminding me that the punch had been real enough, and it was the pain that cleared my head of the disorienting panic.

As he came toward me to deliver the coup de grace, I leapt to one side and brought the side of my hand up in a swinging arc against his Adam's apple. He stood transfixed, momentarily paralyzed, and I measured him for a kick to the solar plexus. My relief as he capsized like a folding deck chair was exhilarating—and right on cue, my success was celebrated with a sudden blaze of light, as the room lights were switched on by Mr. Seeley, standing in the doorway in his dressing gown, holding a hammer he was obviously prepared to use if necessary. I noticed from the clock on the mantelshelf that it was a little after one, and smiled wearily at him as I sat down on the arm of a chair before the approaching giddiness had a chance to overwhelm me.

Assured that I was unhurt, the old man explained apologetically that he had intended to stay awake, but had dozed off and been awakened by the noise. "The whole building seemed to be shaking on its foundations. It wouldn't surprise me if the neighbors downstairs have called the police—it must have sounded like a riot!"

I laughed, realizing it was the first time I had been relaxed enough to laugh naturally since I had started the investigation. "It was close," I admitted. "It doesn't matter if the police turn up now, although I would have preferred to call Paget in my own time. We owe it to ourselves, after all this, to try and get something out of Ingham first."

We remembered the writhing figure on the floor, in considerable pain but otherwise not seriously hurt. I asked Mr. Seeley for cold washcloths and a towel, before hoisting Ingham into an armchair and applying some very basic first aid. Exhausted, the fury in his eyes totally spent, he tried to speak, but I signaled him to keep quiet until we were sure the cold compress had reduced the swelling on his throat.

At that point, there was the sound of a key in a lock outside. The three of us looked simultaneously in the direction of the front door, probably assuming it was the police arriving, although it was not until Norah Peters walked in that I remembered that squad car crews are not issued with the keys to private homes. Norah ignored us, hurried over to Ingham, and pulled the compress away from his throat. "What have they done to you?" she demanded.

I tapped her on the shoulder. "Good evening!" When she did not reply, I added, "I want him to save his voice for more important things. *I'll* tell you what happened—he tried to kill me. Don't worry, he's all right. Where did you get a key?"

She continued to ignore me, more pressingly concerned with satisfying herself Ingham had no concealed injuries. He shook his head reassuringly and smiled at her, and she began to relax.

Mr. Seeley was still uptight about the key. He grabbed her arm and pulled her up, demanding an explanation. She looked down at Ingham for guidance, but I stepped between them to prevent any secret signal. "It's over," I announced. "I was wrong about him from the start. He did kill Jessica. He came back tonight to find this. . . ." I showed her the cross and chain.

I was interrupted by a croaking voice behind me and turned to see Ingham shaking his head in protest. "Not for that reason . . ." he said hoarsely with an effort. "I knew it

was important in some way, although I'm still not sure
how, but I thought if I could steal it, I'd be helping Mrs.
Seeley . . . supporting the burglar theory." He looked from
me to Mr. Seeley appealingly, and I think we both believed
him, but I had realized by now that his truth did not necessarily relate to facts. Having got where we were now
through pressure tactics, I decided to lean on him harder.
"You're a liar!" I shouted. "The *timetable* favors the burglar
theory. But if you had accepted it, you wouldn't have bothered to come looking tonight. You *knew* it was here, because it was you who tore it off and put it back in the
jewelry box!"

He seemed to accept my story, because his shoulders
slumped dispiritedly and he made no attempt to defend
himself. But he still had a champion in Norah. Her expression was pathetically devoted as she moved in front of him
protectingly, like a guard dog. "You're wrong again . . .
you and your wild assumptions," she told me. "I killed
her!"

I was operating now like a computer, too locked into a
fact-finding program to react emotionally anymore; nothing would have surprised me. Mr. Seeley reacted as she
must have expected, but Ingham's expression did not
change, as though he already suspected what she was about
to reveal, or was past caring. Impatient for evidence, I ges-
tured for Norah to explain, and she continued, "You asked
about the key—that's where it started. I had a copy made
from Bill's a few weeks ago."

"You were checking up on him?" I asked, but she did not
answer directly, preferring to tell the story in her own way.

"I've loved him for about three years, but I respected his
marriage; I did nothing until his wife walked out . . . when
it seemed natural for us to come together at last. All his

friends deserted him; I was the only one who cared. It was a particularly harrowing period in his life—he told you himself how his interests kept pulling him in opposite directions—but I was able to help in my own small way, and that made me happy.

"But the happier I felt, the greater my subconscious fears it could not last. I had even started with a handicap, catching him on the rebound, and when there was no one else around. I wasn't exactly jealous of Jessica, but I became more and more conscious of the time he was spending with her. I couldn't see *why* he had to visit her so often now that she was cured. At first I would drop hints, and eventually I asked him outright, but even then he didn't give me a straight answer. The only feasible explanation seemed that he was in love with her . . . when she was having physiotherapy three times a week and was making tremendous strides, she couldn't need him anymore. What else was I to think?

"I had the key cut so that I could burst in on them one day, although, even when I collected it from the locksmith, I'd convinced myself I'd never really use it. On this day, though, when he refused to see someone who genuinely needed help, and went to her instead—I couldn't stand the suspense any longer. I was tempted to take the day off, but I had a long-standing lunch date with the librarian of Dublin University, so I decided to come straight here from lunch. I was late, and it must have been just after Doug Leighton left, although I didn't see the estate car he uses. I opened the front door and crept . . ."

"How did you know where Jessica's room was?" I asked.

"I had an insatiable curiosity about anything to do with her. I pumped Bill at every opportunity, so I had a pretty good picture of the family, how they lived, and even the layout of the flat."

"So you burst straight in, as you'd always imagined?"

She smiled. "These things never work out the way we imagine. Even at that late stage, I hesitated. If I had heard them talking normally I'm sure I would have chickened out, perhaps compromised by going out again and ringing the bell . . . to pretend I had been passing, or anything they might accept. But it was so suspiciously quiet, I *had* to satisfy my curiosity. I didn't bother to knock—just walked in and saw them . . . Bill on the carpet—I assumed, in an exhausted sleep—and her starting to get dressed. It was much worse than I had imagined.

"She was probably startled by my sudden appearance, but recovered her composure almost immediately. She even glanced down at her naked breasts suggestively, to mock me. She must have guessed who I was, but she turned it into a charade, making a wide-eyed pretense at apologizing for what I had witnessed, saying that they had tried to control their feelings for each other, but . . . she was so obviously baiting me that I lost my temper and slapped her face. But she was stronger than I anticipated; she grabbed my arm and twisted it. I lost my balance and fell against her, and the warmth of her flesh reminded me of what had probably happened before I arrived.

"I had an aversion to touching her, so I reached out blindly for something to defend myself with. My fingers found the candlestick and I aimed at her shoulder, but in the heat of the moment a couple of blows landed on her head. It was only when she went limp that I realized how hard they must have been."

"And so you panicked and left?" I commented.

"Yes—I must have done."

"What about leaving Bill behind to face the music?"

"I tried to revive him, but he just groaned and went back to sleep. Anyway, I admit I was angry at the way he had betrayed me. I thought it would serve him right—trying to explain how she had been hurt. I didn't know she was dying."

"You wanted to punish him—but changed your mind later?"

"I love him. When I heard his side of the story, I was more than ever convinced that *she* seduced *him*. Besides, by then I knew she was dead and that he was not to blame."

"But why didn't you tell your story to the police when they arrested him?" I asked.

"They didn't actually arrest him at first, just detained him for questioning, and I didn't believe they could build a watertight case. But if he was committed for trial, I would have given myself up."

I didn't believe her. Norah fitted my image of Lady Bountiful, the noble heroine only too willing to sacrifice herself for the man she loved. "What happened to the cross round her neck?"

"It came off in the struggle."

"And what did you do with it?"

She shook her head in confusion. "I can't remember *everything*. It all happened so quickly."

I asked her to reenact the scene, with me playing the part of Jessica. Mr. Seeley was still holding the hammer he had brought in with him. I handed it over and asked her to place me in the correct position. With a minimum of hesitation, she directed me to a chair, and then, rather self-consciously, holding the hammer in her right hand, simulated a clubbing blow at my head. I had a momentary qualm that she might really connect, but trusted that the presence of Seeley and

Ingham would restrain any such inclination. She stopped the blow an inch or so from my hair.

Her expression was very intense, but when I reminded her that Jessica had allegedly twisted her arm, it turned to irritation, the look implying that details were unimportant. However, when she dutifully folded her left arm behind her back, I easily held it in position, pointing out that my left hand was still free to counter the weapon hand. She shook her head in confusion. "What difference does it make?" she said irritably.

"You can't remember, because it never happened," I said. "The injuries to her head were mainly on the left side, which means they could have been inflicted by your right hand—at close quarters."

I returned the hammer to Mr. Seeley and asked if he had a candlestick to match the one retained by the police. He nodded and went out while I turned to Ingham, who was still sitting dispiritedly in the armchair. He looked up at me with that irritatingly earnest expression and asked, "It has to be me, doesn't it?"

"You *are* left-handed, aren't you?" I replied. "That's why you caught me with that wild swing. I was always a sucker for a southpaw."

Seeley returned with the candlestick and placed it in Ingham's left hand. I asked him to keep looking at it until he was blindfolded, explaining that, in the absence of Sir Robert Cheatle, I was going to try a less orthodox but equally scientific experiment. I borrowed Norah's chiffon scarf and tied it round his eyes. "I want you to think back to that afternoon, keeping the picture of the candlestick in your mind," I instructed him.

Waiting until he was sufficiently engrossed in the flashback, I signaled Seeley to switch on the tape recorder we had concealed. The sound of Jessica's voice shattered the silence, frightening and disturbing us all, but effective as a spotlight and rubber truncheon in laying bare Ingham's buried memories. The voice was vibrant, persuasive and demanding.

". . . Mark . . . why did you do it? I loved you . . . Mark Kingdom, God blessed you with healing hands . . . please, bring me back to life. I want you. . . !"

I watched him closely, watched the knuckles whiten as they gripped the candlestick, the whole body stiffen, and suddenly the explosion of fury again as he leapt to his feet, one hand tearing at the scarf round his eyes, the other brandishing the candlestick as he advanced in the direction of the disembodied voice. As the blindfold came away, he stopped in his tracks, blinking sharply at the light, and wondering where Jessica had gone. The anger dropped as sharply as mercury, and he turned to me in confusion, but with evident relief that the memory block had at last been removed. He handed me back the candlestick and asked how I had staged the phony séance.

"It was an edited extract from your first public appearance," I said. "I remembered Leighton's account, about how impressive Jessica had been, so I borrowed it, and for once in our relationship he made himself useful. We got one of his contacts, a recording-studio engineer, to make a copy, cut out key words, and put them together again in the form of a fake message. The intonation wasn't always spot on—but I didn't think you'd notice in the circumstances!"

He smiled wryly. "It was good enough. I'm afraid I wasted your time during the past week, Matt." He turned to Mr. Seeley. "I'm sorry . . . particularly that it took so long to come to my senses, and that we couldn't have spared your wife her ordeal."

Seeley said nothing, but I knew he appreciated the sentiment. Ingham then thanked Norah for her compassion and
blind faith in him. "I don't deserve it," he said without any
trace of self-pity.

"She drove you to it," Norah argued desperately.

He shook his head. "It's not true. I'm not just saying this
to spare Mr. Seeley's feelings—but I'm as guilty as hell."
He turned to me to complete his story. "There's no point in
going right back. Let's start with the pictures. They set me
up, as Leighton told you. As I recovered, the first thing I
saw was her face leaning over me. When my senses cleared,
I realized she was partially undressed. I recall being excited
and too drowsy to care about hiding my feelings anymore.
She was smiling and I somehow took it for granted from our
respective positions that we had been making love. The realization was like an orgasm, a tremendous relief. Suddenly I
knew the truth. I loved her; I had never loved anyone else in
this way; never would. At the same time the knowledge
filled me with shame and anger at the way I had finally
allowed my conscience to be subjugated, even humiliated.

"It must have been that traumatic realization that set up
the memory block; why the amnesia started *before* her death.
I know now that my shame was suicidal. And it was when
she realized that, and that I was slipping away from her
again, that she told me what had really happened, and how
she intended to exploit the new hold over me. What an
irony! Little did she realize she had accomplished what she
intended—without needing the photographs! But that's like
crying over spilled milk. You see, I loved Jessica *despite* the
evil side to her nature, but at that moment I was only concerned about the injustice of it all. I saw red and grabbed her
by the throat.

"With my hands on her flesh I felt calm again, merely

indignant at the way she had repaid me for curing her. It seemed only fair that if God had given me the authority to restore life to her legs, he should permit me to take it back . . . she was unworthy.

"She struggled. Norah guessed correctly when she said Jessica was strong . . . because she had learned to depend on her arms. . . . She grabbed the candlestick and started hitting me about the head and shoulders. I had expected her to understand my point of view, but when she hit me I must have gone berserk. I wrestled it from her grip and smashed it down on her head. I remember seeing the glow of red and orange sparks trailing from the brightness of the candlestick, like the fiery passing of meteorites in the atmosphere, but on reflection I suppose that must have been a residue of the LSD effects. I'm not pretending that had anything to do with my actions.

"I honestly intended to kill myself rather than impose a long-drawn-out trial on my friends. But almost immediately my memory started playing tricks. By the time I was leaving I was starting to wonder what she was doing on the floor. It must have been an instinct for self-preservation that drove me away, although I was only vaguely aware of why I was running. The rest you know."

"My heart *bleeds* for you," I declared, my tone heavy with sarcasm. "Sounds like an open-and-shut case of self-defense. . . ."

Ingham was confused by my reaction. "It's what happened. I'd blotted out the memory until tonight, but I'm not trying to hide anything now. . . ."

"That may be so, but what gets up my nose is the air of martyrdom—as though you were the victim of circumstances. . . ."

"I've accepted the responsibility for Jessica's death from

the beginning. All I've added is that I didn't realize until
tonight that I was actually the instrument."

"There may well have been mitigating circumstances, but
you've conveniently forgotten the attempt to kill Laura—
that was in cold blood. You're not going to deny that, I
hope?"

He shook his head. "How did you know?"

"Because when you phoned you expected to speak to me.
You couldn't have known whether or not I'd made contact
with Magda in Paris, so it had to be a lifelike impression,
and I remember George Kester saying that you had a talent
for impersonating celebrities. It wouldn't have been difficult
to copy your wife's voice, especially over the phone. Why
did you do it?"

He shrugged. "It should have been you, of course. I
didn't count on Laura turning up. . . ."

"But you had only just professed your undying gratitude,
or some such bullshit, for the way I had helped you. . . ."

"That was Bill Ingham—who meant every word. It was
Mark Kingdom who recognized the fresh threat over the
missing necklace. It was he who set the trap at the bindery."

"And who is speaking now?"

His smile was ironic. "It began with a struggle for control, with the two clearly defined personalities taking it in
turns to take over—at which stage the one in the ascen-
dancy was not even aware of the other's existence. You
mentioned Jekyll and Hyde before; that's exactly it. It has
come full circle, and now it is too late, I can rationalize the
situation. Not an admission my defense lawyer will want to
hear, but it's the truth."

Drummond was unhappy. Even the sop of a second major exclusive in less than a week failed to improve his dis-

position. It seemed I had upset the applecart, interfered with the status quo he coveted, and I was treated to his entire range of pained expressions, sighs, winces, and teeth sucking, as he wondered why he had allowed me to talk him into becoming involved.

I sighed with relief that I was no longer part of Drummond's circle, that I could get back to a world where moral values counted for something. Even Laura, who had joined me in Ardley for the weekend, commented on the uplifting quality of the place. A week in London had been enough.

I was also back with Wilkie Collins. As I climbed into bed, I removed the bookmark on page 59 and it was as though I had not been away. The yellow circle of my bedside lamp assisted the atmosphere I sought, but in the shadows beyond I could make out a hauntingly lovely vision in a white nightgown. I looked up sharply—but it was Laura; there was nothing unearthly about Laura. For a split second I thought of Wilkie Collins' woman in white, but compelling though she might be, I knew where my true preference lay. I closed the book and reached out a hand.

F
LEW   Lewis, Roy Harley.

           Miracles take a
             little longer

$14.95

DATE			